Jonathan
Edwards

*The unwavering Resolve of
Jonathan Edwards
by Steve Lawson*

WOMEN OF FAITH SERIES

Amy Carmichael	*Harriet Tubman*
Catherine Marshall	*Isobel Kuhn*
Corrie ten Boom	*Joni*
Fanny Crosby	*Madame Guyon*
Florence Nightingale	*Mary Slessor*
Gladys Aylward	*Susanna Wesley*

MEN OF FAITH SERIES

Andrew Murray	*John Calvin*
Borden of Yale	*John Hyde*
Brother Andrew	*John Newton*
C. S. Lewis	*John Paton*
Charles Colson	*John Wesley*
Charles Finney	*Jonathan Edwards*
Charles Spurgeon	*Jonathan Goforth*
D. L. Moody	*Luis Palau*
David Brainerd	*Martin Luther*
E. M. Bounds	*Oswald Chambers*
Eric Liddell	*Samuel Morris*
George Muller	*William Booth*
Hudson Taylor	*William Carey*
Jim Elliot	

WOMEN AND MEN OF FAITH

John and Betty Stam
Francis and Edith Schaeffer

OTHER BIOGRAPHIES FROM BETHANY HOUSE

Autobiography of Charles Finney
George MacDonald: Scotland's Beloved Storyteller
Hannah Whitall Smith
Janette Oke: A Heart for the Prairie
Miracle in the Mirror (Nita Edwards)
Of Whom the World Was Not Worthy (Jakob Kovac family)

MEN OF FAITH

Jonathan Edwards

David J. Vaughan

BETHANY HOUSE PUBLISHERS
MINNEAPOLIS, MINNESOTA 55438

Jonathan Edwards
Copyright © 2000
David J. Vaughan

Cover illustration by Joe Nordstrom

Library of Congress Catalog Card Number 99–006868

ISBN 0–7642–2168-X

Published by Bethany House Publishers
A Ministry of Bethany Fellowship International
11400 Hampshire Avenue South
Minneapolis, Minnesota 55438
www.bethanyhouse.com

Printed in the United States of America by
Bethany Press International, Minneapolis, Minnesota
55438

DAVID VAUGHAN is pastor of Liberty Christian Church and director of Liberty Leadership Institute. A graduate of the University of Missouri—St. Louis, he holds a Ph.D. from Whitefield Theological Seminary. David's many accomplishments include being a writer, editor, speaker, and community leader. He and his wife and their four children make their home in Missouri.

Acknowledgments

Of the many friends who have supported me over the years, special thanks go to the staff of Liberty Christian Church: Tim and Kim Ward, Jim and Cathy Cummings, David and Katherine Volz, and Bryan and Debbie Short. To the members of Liberty, I can only say that it is a privilege to serve you as pastor.

Thanks also to George Grant for launching my writing career, and to Steve Laube of Bethany House for recruiting me for this project.

Most important, I am indebted to my wife, Diane, and to my children, Hannah, Lydia, Ethan, and Adam. May each of you learn the secret of consecration.

Contents

1

The Puritan Hope

The great experiment of American theocracy was coming to a close at the time of Jonathan Edwards' birth in 1703. The fire of our Puritan forefathers was cooling to a smoldering ember. As the zeal of genuine piety waned, many decried the decline in religion and bewailed the spiritual apathy that pervaded the Colonies. In 1706 Cotton Mather, like Jeremiah of old, poured out his lamentation:

> It is confessed by all who know anything of the matter . . . that there is a general and an horrible decay of Christianity, among the professors of it. . . . The modern Christianity is too generally but a very spectre, scarce a shadow of the ancient. Ah! Sinful nation. Ah! Children that are corrupters: what have your hands done![1]

Mather was not alone in drawing a depressing picture of Colonial carnality. "The ministerial utterances of the period—from the pulpit and press—were equally gloomy."[2] Richard Webster repined: "A vast change was visible in the churches of New England: the discipline was relaxed, the doctrine was diluted, and the preaching tame and spiritless."[3] Just a year before Edwards' birth, Increase Mather wistfully recalled the glory of earlier days: "You that are aged, and can remember what New England was fifty years ago, that saw these churches in their first glory, is there not a sad decay and diminution of that glory! How is the gold become dim!"[4] For the most part, religion had sunk to a new low in the Colonies. As one historian noted:

> Taken as a whole, no century in American religious history has been so barren as the eighteenth. The fire and enthusiasm of Puritanism had died out on both sides of the Atlantic. In this country the inevitable provincialism of the narrow colonial life, the deadening influence of its hard grapple with the rude forces of nature, and the Indian and Canadian wars rendered each generation less actively religious than its predecessor; and, while New England shone as compared with the spiritual deadness of Old England in the years preceding Wesley, the old fervor and sense of a national mission were gone, conscious conversion, once so common, was unusual, and religion was becoming more formal and external.[5]

In addition to the reasons just mentioned, other factors facilitated the decline of Puritan piety. One was the development of the Half-Way Covenant. As the second generation of Puritans grew up in Christian homes, many were converted but could not give an explicit account of their conversion experience, a requirement for full membership in the church. As "noncommunicant" members they could neither vote nor partake of the Lord's Supper. But what about their children? Could noncommunicant parents present their children for baptism? In 1656 a group of New England clergymen met in Boston to debate the question. Their solution, known as the Half-Way Covenant, stated that children of noncommunicant members could be baptized provided the children led a morally

upright life and agreed to profess the church covenant
before the congregation. These children essentially
became "half-way" church members like their parents. As adults, they in turn had their children baptized under the same conditions. To compound the
compromise, Solomon Stoddard of Northampton (Jonathan Edwards' own grandfather) advanced the idea
that these "half-way" members should be offered full
Communion, believing that the Lord's Supper was a
means of conversion. Thus the visible church was in-
filtrated by people who made no profession of saving
faith. The sad but inevitable result was the decay of
spiritual vitality.

Edwards' own parents were, however, a notable ex-
ception to the prevailing decline. His father, Timothy
Edwards, a man of fair complexion, strong build, and
lively temperament, was a genuinely godly man. As
pastor of the church in East Windsor, Connecticut,
Timothy's ministry had been graced with several seasons of revival. As Jonathan was to write much later:

> My honoured father's parish has in times past
> been a place favoured with mercies of this [awaken-
> ing] nature, above any on this western side of New
> England, excepting Northampton; there having been
> four or five seasons of the pouring out of the Spirit to
> the general awakening of the people there since my
> father's settlement amongst them.[6]

It was some years earlier, when Timothy was a student at Harvard, that he met his future bride, Esther
Stoddard, who would become the mother of Jonathan.
Esther was a woman of great grace and wit: tall, af-
fable, and, according to some, even superior to her
husband in "native vigour of understanding."[7] The
Stoddards were one of the leading families in the Connecticut Valley due to the influence of Esther's father,

the Reverend Solomon Stoddard, who began a long and powerful ministry at Northampton in 1669. In the course of his extended pastorate (1669 to 1729), the city of Northampton became the largest city of inland Massachusetts, and Stoddard's reputation as a preacher grew apace with the city.

On November 6, 1694, Timothy Edwards married Esther Stoddard at Northampton, and a week later they moved to East Windsor, where Timothy had been called to preach. After an initial probation period he was ordained pastor in March 1695. Since the General Court had only recently authorized the organization of a separate parish, the people were busy constructing a new meetinghouse and parsonage. Timothy's own father, Richard Edwards, covered the cost of the brick and hewn timber and purchased some surrounding farmland for the newlyweds.

Here, in the two-story log parsonage, Jonathan Edwards was born on October 5, 1703. The only son of eleven children (four sisters preceded him and six sisters followed), Jonathan was naturally of special interest to his father. Since there was no school in the fledgling East Windsor, Timothy Edwards schooled his children at home; and, like other New England ministers, he often took in students from the surrounding area. Having graduated from Harvard with both a bachelor's and a master's degree, he was, of course, eminently qualified to do so. In addition to a thorough knowledge of the Bible and Reformed theology, Timothy excelled in the Greek and Latin classics and had a fondness for poetry and the study of nature.

Under his father's tutelage, Jonathan began the study of Latin at the age of six, and by the age of thirteen he had a reading knowledge of Latin, Greek, and

Hebrew. He also was taught to study at all times with a pen in his hand. This habit, begun at an early age, trained Edwards to think clearly and logically and to store up his reflections on many important subjects. His father's love of nature was also passed on to him. It was not uncommon for Jonathan to lie on the green grass outside his home and watch flying insects, such as butterflies or moths, or to stroll in the woods and patiently observe the operations of "flying" spiders. In fact, at the mere age of eleven, the young naturalist wrote a three-thousand-word "scientific" paper on the spider. Some years later Edwards reworked the original and submitted it to the Royal Society of London. Although it was never published, it does show Edwards' precocious gifts of observation and analysis. Edwards' genius is reflected in the well-known anecdote of Professor H. C. McCook, who believed himself the first person to make certain observations on the flying spider. He was chagrined to learn that Edwards had anticipated him by 160 years.

More important, Jonathan learned from his father, as well as his mother, a high view of God the Father, Christ, the Bible, and the Christian ministry. His home was the scene of many devout prayers and divine precepts. Both parents set a godly example that only served to reinforce their parental instruction. Their hearts' desire was that their son "might be filled with the Holy Spirit; from a child know the Holy Scriptures; and be great in the sight of the Lord."[8]

His father was an earnest preacher whose ministry saw the blessing of God's Spirit in several seasons of "reviving of religion." During one of these general awakenings the Holy Spirit touched Jonathan himself. As he later wrote:

I had a variety of concerns and exercises about my soul from my childhood; but I had two more remarkable seasons of awakening before I met with that change by which I was brought to those new dispositions, and that new sense of things, that I have since had. The first time was when I was a boy, some years before I went to College, at a time of remarkable awakening in my father's congregation. I was very much affected for many months, and concerned about the things of religion, and my soul's salvation. . . . I used to pray five times a day in secret, and to spend much time in religious talk with other boys; and used to meet with them to pray together. I experienced I know not what kind of delight in religion. My mind was much engaged in it, and had much self-righteous pleasure, and it was my delight to abound in religious duties.[9]

Jonathan joined together with some schoolmates and built a prayer booth in a retired place in a swamp, and would often go to secret places in the woods by himself to pray. Although he was "much affected" at this time, Edwards believed that his real conversion was to come later. Eventually his "convictions and affections wore off" and he "went on in the ways of sin."[10]

Nevertheless, his father had fortified him intellectually and stimulated him spiritually. He was now ready to venture out into the world as a young scholar. Thus, at the tender age of thirteen, Jonathan Edwards headed for Yale.

2

Meeting God at Yale

E dwards joined the Collegiate School of Connecticut (later called Yale) in the autumn of 1716. The school charter, drawn up in 1701, succinctly stated the goal and vision of its founders: "to promote the power and piety of religion, and the best edification of these New England Churches."[1] In contrast to the liberal-leaning Harvard, the school was committed to conserving the Puritan heritage of New England. Thus its founders filled the original library with weighty Reformers like Alsted, Wollebius, and other Dutch and Swiss theologians.

Being in its infancy, the college had no official name. It also had no official location, a fact that led to controversy among the students, teachers, and trustees. When Edwards began his collegiate career, there were student bodies in four different locations: Saybrook, New Haven, Wethersfield, and Hartford. In the midst of much wrangling between parents and trustees, it was decided, in October 1716, that the permanent site of the college would be New Haven. Despite this decision, Edwards and a group of students stayed at Wethersfield, under the instruction of Elisha Williams, Edwards' half-cousin. It was not until two years later that the General Assembly of Connecticut, in October 1718, resolved tensions, and the Wethersfield students moved to New Haven in the summer of 1719. Thus Edwards was absent from the commencement ceremonies of September 1718, when the school was officially named Yale.

The curriculum at young Yale was a blend of traditional Reformed theology and what was then being called the "new learning"—the philosophy of Descartes, Boyle, Locke, and Newton. In general, the four-year course covered ancient languages (Latin, Greek, and Hebrew), logic, natural science, higher mathematics, and some astronomy. Writing home to his father, Jonathan requested help in acquiring some of the needed texts and supplies:

> I have inquired of Mr. Cutler what books we shall need of the next year. He answered, he would have me to get against that time, Alstead's Geometry and Gassendus's Astronomy; with which I would entreat you to get a pair of dividers, or mathematician's compasses, and a scale, which are absolutely necessary in order to learning mathematics; and also the Art of Thinking, which, I am persuaded, would be no less profitable than the other necessary. . . .[2]

Since the primary aim of the school was to train godly ministers and to promote the welfare of the churches in New England, courses in divinity, homiletics, New Testament Greek, and the Hebrew Psalter were also assigned. Moreover, students had to memorize the Westminster Catechism and the Theological Theses (*Marrow of Sacred Theology*) of William Ames.

The spiritual life of the students was encouraged also. The "Orders and Appointments" for the students included the following regimen:

> Every student shall exercise himself in reading
> the Holy Scriptures by himself every day that the
> word of Christ may dwell in him richly. . . . All stu-
> dents shall avoid the profanation of God's holy name,
> attributes, Word and ordinances and the Holy Sab-
> bath, and shall carefully attend all public assemblies
> for divine worship. . . . All undergraduates shall pub-
> licly repeat sermons in the hall in their course,
> and . . . be constantly examined on Sabbaths at eve-
> ning prayer. . . .[3]

Edwards' education served him well. Being naturally precocious and curious, he studied hard and finished his undergraduate work first in his class. In
September 1720 he gave the farewell oration at the
college commencement exercises. However, instead of
heading home, he stayed at Yale to pursue his master's degree.

The years 1720 to 1726 were critical in Edwards'
intellectual and spiritual development. As a graduate
student (1720–1722) and later as a tutor (1724–1726),
Edwards' intellectual horizons were greatly ex-
panded. He read the "new learning" with great avid-
ity. His favorite philosopher at the time was John
Locke, whose *Essay Concerning Human Understanding* gave him more pleasure "than the most greedy
miser finds when gathering up handfuls of silver and
gold."[4]

Because Edwards had learned to study with pen in
hand, he began at this time his lifelong practice of
keeping manuscript "notebooks" with such headings
as "Natural Philosophy," "The Mind," "Miscellanies,"
and others. In his "Notes on Natural Science," Edwards demonstrates an understanding and appreciation of Newton, not to mention the genius of his own
scientific mind. He discusses, for instance, the definition of an atom, its constitution, gravity, repulsion,

and attraction; light, color; planets, comets; the growth of trees; lightning, the twinkling of fixed stars; how water freezes or evaporates, etc. And in another essay, "Of Being," he argues for the inevitability of existence from the inconceivability of nonexistence.

One such notebook, entitled "Catalogues," listed the books that Edwards had read or wanted to read. Of the 690 entries, 452 were on religious subjects. From this list it is clear that his favorite authors were the older Puritans, such as William Perkins, Richard Sibbes, Thomas Manton, John Flavel, John Owen, Stephen Charnock, and others. He was also conversant with Calvin, Turretin, and van Mastricht; the latter, he said, being "better than any other book in the world, excepting the Bible, in my opinion."[5]

Edwards' spiritual growth was, of course, even more consequential than his intellectual development. Although he had previously been touched by the Spirit of God when a child, Edwards was going through a crisis of faith. Despite his efforts to live in a godly manner, he found that he repeatedly suffered "inward struggles and conflicts" of temptation. He now began to see that true Christianity was more than mere external conformity to a set of rules. He needed a deep and abiding change within his heart. He started to seek salvation with a new fervor. "I was indeed brought to seek salvation in a manner that I never was before; I felt a spirit to part with all things in the world for an interest in Christ."[6]

Like the "wretched man" of Romans, Edwards finally surrendered his self-effort and cried out to God for deliverance. In the late spring of 1721 his prayer was graciously answered. As he later wrote in his *Personal Narrative*, he entered the joy and peace of salvation while one day reading 1 Timothy 1:17:

The instance that I remember of that sort of inward, sweet delight in God and divine things that I have lived much in since, was on reading those words, 1 Tim. 1:17, "Now unto the King eternal, immortal, invisible, the only wise God, be and glory for ever and ever, Amen." As I read the words, there came into my soul, and was as it were diffused through it, a sense of the glory of the Divine Being; a new sense, quite different from anything I ever experienced before. . . . I thought with myself, how excellent a Being that was, and how happy I should be, if I might enjoy that God, and be rapt up in him in heaven, and be as it were swallowed up in him for ever![7]

From then on Edwards began to have new "apprehensions and ideas" about Christ, redemption, and salvation. "An inward, sweet sense of these things, at times, came into my heart; and my soul was led away in pleasant views and contemplations of them." Edwards was enraptured with Christ himself and would spend many hours "reading and meditating on Christ, on the beauty and excellency of his person, and the lovely way of salvation by free grace." The Song of Solomon became his favorite. While meditating upon it a sense of divine things "would often of a sudden kindle up . . . a sweet burning in my heart; an ardor of soul, that I know not how to express."[8]

That summer Edwards returned home and shared his spiritual experience with his father. After their conversation, which "much affected" Edwards, he went out into his father's pasture to meditate:

And as I was walking there, and looking up on the sky and clouds, there came into my mind so sweet a sense of the glorious *majesty* and *grace* of God, that I know not how to express—I seemed to see them both in a sweet conjunction; majesty and meekness joined together. . . .

Clearly Edwards was in the honeymoon glow of his

conversion: that sweet and joyous time of experiencing "all things new" in Christ. "The appearance of every thing was altered; there seemed to be, as it were, a calm, sweet cast, or appearance of divine glory, in almost everything." Even nature was aglow with the glory of God. "God's excellency, his wisdom, his purity and love, seemed to appear in everything; in the sun, moon, and stars; in the clouds, and blue sky; in the grass, flowers, trees; in the water and all nature; which used greatly to fix my mind."[9]

While spending the summer at home he would often spend hours contemplating the handiwork of God in creation. He would observe the sky and clouds while "singing forth, with a low voice my contemplations of the Creator and Redeemer." Whereas Edwards used to be terrified by thunder, he now rejoiced in it as a manifestation of God's powerful and majestic voice. Indeed, whenever a storm approached he would perch himself in a location where he could best view the coming glory, and while gazing up at God's fireworks he would "break forth in singing or chanting" his meditations.[10]

When Edwards returned to Yale in the autumn of 1721, he was not content to be a nominal Christian. As he later wrote, "I felt then great satisfaction, as to my good state; but that did not content me. I had vehement longings of soul after God and Christ, and after more holiness, wherewith my heart seemed to be full, and ready to break. . . ."[11] He was determined to devote himself entirely to God. Indeed this is the key to understanding the power and life of Edwards. And this is undoubtedly the reason why God in His providence was to later use him as a mighty instrument of revival. His intention to fully consecrate himself to God can be seen in the following "Resolutions," which he began writing in 1722 while at Yale:

Being sensible that I am unable to do anything without God's help, I do humbly entreat him by his grace to enable me to keep these Resolutions, so far as they are agreeable to his will, for Christ's sake:

Resolved, that I will do whatsoever I think to be most to God's glory, and my own good, profit and pleasure in the whole of my duration [life], without any consideration of the time, whether now, or ever so many myriads of ages hence. Resolved to do whatever I think to be my duty and most for the good and advantage of mankind in general. Resolved to do this, whatever difficulties I meet with, how many soever, and how great soever.

Resolved, never to do any manner of thing, whether in soul or body, less or more, but what tends to the glory of God; not be, nor suffer it, if I can avoid it.

Resolved, never to do anything, which I should be afraid to do, if it were the last hour of my life.

Resolved, when I feel pain, to think of the pains of martyrdom, and of hell.

Resolved, to be endeavoring to find out fit objects of charity and liberality.

Resolved, to live so, at all times, as I think is best in my devout frames, and when I have clearest notions of things of the gospel, and another world.

Resolved, to examine carefully, and constantly, what that one thing in me is, which causes me in the least to doubt of the love of God; and to direct all my forces against it.

Resolved, to study the Scriptures so steadily, constantly and frequently, as that I may find, and plainly perceive myself to grow in knowledge of the same.

Resolved, to strive to my utmost every week to be brought higher in religion, and to a higher exercise of grace, than I was the week before.

Resolved, never to say anything at all against anybody, but when it is perfectly agreeable to the highest degree of Christian honor, and of love to mankind, agreeable to the lowest humility, and a sense of my own faults and failings, and agreeable to the golden rule. . . .[12]

While Edwards was penning his "Resolutions," he received a call to preach in New York to a small Presbyterian church. Accordingly, he was licensed for the work of the ministry, dropped his MA studies at Yale, and headed for New York, where he settled in August 1722.

Edwards' early sermons overflowed with his new-found life in Christ: "When a man is enlightened savingly by Christ, he is, as it were, brought into a new world. . . ." As he himself had experienced, the new convert now "sees with his own eyes and admires and is astonished" at the "excellency of religion and the glorious mysteries of the gospel." He loves Christ more than any other lover: "there is no such near or intimate conversation between any other lovers as between Christ and the Christian."[13] This was certainly true of Christ and Edwards. As he wrote later, while at New York his desire for Christ and holiness only intensified:

> My sense of divine things seemed gradually to increase, until I went to preach at New York, which was about a year and a half after they began; and while I was there, I felt them, very sensible, in a much higher degree than I had done before. My longing after God and holiness, were much increased. Pure and humble, holy and heavenly, Christianity appeared exceeding amiable to me.

Edwards now "felt a burning desire to be in every thing a complete Christian; and conformed to the blessed image of Christ; and that I might live, in all things, according to the pure, sweet and blessed rules of the gospel."[14]

"God and holiness!" "Christ and holiness!" These ideas are inseparably linked in Edwards' mind and experience. To have the one is to possess the other. Holiness is not a burdensome duty, however; it is the beautiful condition of the soul in communion with God. Here is how Edwards, in one of his more eloquent passages, then described it:

> Holiness ... appeared to me to be of a sweet, pleasant, charming serene, calm nature; which brought an inexpressible purity, brightness, peacefulness and ravishment to the soul. In other words, that it made the soul like a field or garden of God, with all manner of pleasant flowers; all pleasant, delightful, and undisturbed; enjoying a sweet calm, and the gentle vivifying beams of the sun. The soul of a true Christian, as I then wrote ... appeared like such a little white flower as we see in the spring of the year; low and humble on the ground, opening its bosom to receive the pleasant beams of the sun's glory; rejoicing as it were in a calm rapture; diffusing around a sweet fragrance. ... There is no part of creature holiness, that I had so great a sense of its loveliness, as humility, brokenness of heart and poverty of spirit; and there was nothing that I so earnestly longed for. My heart panted after this—to lie low before God, as in the dust; that I might be nothing, and God might be all. ...[15]

Edwards' ardent passion for God issued in a decisive act of self-consecration. On the morning of January 12, 1723, he was again alone with God. In this solitary place of communion he "solemnly renewed" his self-dedication. Standing before God alone, without the acknowledgment or praise of men, Edwards vowed complete self-renunciation and devotion to God. As he wrote in his diary:

> I have been before God; and have given myself, all that I am and have to God, so that I am not in any

respect my own: I can challenge no right in myself, I
can challenge no right in this understanding, this
will, these affections that are in me; neither have I
any right to this body, any of its members: no right to
this tongue, these hands nor feet: no right to these
senses, these eyes, these ears, this smell or taste. I
have given myself clear away, and have not retained
anything as my own. I have been to God this morning,
and told him that I have given myself *wholly* to him.
I have given every power to him; so that for the future
I will challenge no right in myself, in any respect. . . .
This have I done. And I pray God, for the sake of
Christ, to look upon it as a self-dedication; and to receive me now as entirely his own, and deal with me
in all respects as such, whether he afflicts me or pros-
pers me, or whatever he pleases to do with me, who
am his.[16]

Biographer Iain Murray is right when he says that
Edwards' *Resolutions* and *Diary*, written at this time,
give us "the key to the understanding of his whole life
and future ministry. . . . His endeavors after holiness
are no more the self-conscious strivings of a moralist:
rather they are the response of love to the God who
had made him a new creature in Jesus Christ." Sanctification was now a labor of love flowing from "communion with God and fellowship with Christ."[17] Moreover, Edwards' solemn self-dedication was perhaps
the most significant private act he ever made; for God
clearly heard his prayer and deigned to employ him as
one of the mightiest preachers in the history of the
church.

Edwards' stay in New York was a time of heaven
on earth. Yet it was cut short by the congregation's
lack of financial resources. They could not afford either the building upkeep or Edwards' salary. Thus in
April 1723 after only an eight-month pastorate, he de-
parted disconsolate from his little New York flock. "My

heart seemed to sink within me," he later wrote, "at leaving the family and city where I had enjoyed so many sweet and pleasant days. . . . As I sailed away, I kept sight of the city as long as I could; and when I was out of sight of it, it would affect me much to look that way, with a kind of melancholy mixed with sweetness."[18]

Throughout the summer of 1723 Edwards preached at various churches and finished up his MA thesis. And in September he was awarded his graduate degree, a month shy of his twentieth birthday.[19] He was now being pursued as a pastor and as a scholar. While calls were coming in from several New England churches where he had preached, Yale offered him a position as a tutor. But Edwards' desire was to be in the pulpit. His heart was foremost in the ministry and his new master passion was the study and exposition of God's Word.

Edwards' father, on the other hand, pressed him to return to Yale. Perhaps he believed Jonathan would benefit from the academic environment at Yale, or it may have been because of the recent defection or "apostasy" of the Yale faculty. In 1722 both Timothy Cutler, the rector, and another tutor, Daniel Brown, denounced Congregationalism, resigned from Yale, and sought Anglican ordination in England. This event caused great concern at the time and was viewed as evidence of the growing threat of Arminianism and Episcopalianism. The school was floundering and needed brilliant young men like Edwards "to help repair the shattered prestige of the college."[20] So, somewhat reluctantly, Edwards deferred to his father and returned to Yale in June of 1724.

The next two years were a spiritual wasteland for Edwards. While he increased in intellectual knowledge, he decreased in spiritual comfort. In fact, in his *Personal Narrative*, he sums up his time as a tutor by such dismal remarks as "After I went to New Haven, I sunk in religion; my mind being diverted from my eager and violent pursuits after holiness. . . ." Later, after a severe illness in September 1725, Edwards observes, "I was again greatly diverted in my mind . . . to the wounding of my soul. . . ."[21] Despite his inward struggles, Edwards performed his duties admirably. He and his fellow tutors were later recognized as "the pillar tutors, and the glory of the college. . . . Their tutorial renown was great and excellent."[22]

Fortunately, God remembered His struggling servant. In August of 1726 Edwards received a call to minister as the associate pastor of his maternal grandfather, Solomon Stoddard. A month later he gladly resigned from Yale and hastened to Northampton.

3

Northampton: Ministry and Marriage

E dwards' ministry at Northampton began with the brightness of a New England summer sun. Yet over the peaceful horizon a dark storm was stirring. Little did Edwards know that the dissension and strife that would one day spring up and poison his own ministry already lay festering.

It was the rich and fertile soil of Northampton that first attracted settlers to this fortified village in 1650. Except for a few trades and professional people, the majority of the town's inhabitants lived off the land. The men rose at dawn to a simple breakfast of bread and cornmeal pudding, labored until the church bell rang at noon for lunch, and resumed their work till dusk. After a supper of meat, bread, and milk, the typical Northampton family had a time of prayer and Bible reading before going to bed for the night. Life in Northampton was a common round of routines reminiscent of Longfellow's village blacksmith:

> Toiling—rejoicing—sorrowing,
> Onward through life he goes;
> Each morning sees some task begin,

Each evening sees it close;
Something attempted, something done,
Has earned a night's repose.[1]

The people of Northampton were knit together by several facts of Colonial life: social friendships, common lands, the development of common schools, the need for a militia, and most important, their common worship of God. The daily routine of work was punctuated by the weekly ritual of worship. The Sabbath began on Saturday evening, with worship services on Sunday morning and afternoon. An additional "lecture" was also attended on Thursday afternoons at two o'clock. The form of service included praise from *The Bay Psalm Book*, pastor-led prayer, and a lengthy (sometimes two-hour) sermon.

Between 1670 and 1729 the population of Northampton grew from five hundred to over fifteen hundred; and due to the scarce and expensive land, it became a closed, homogeneous community. Writing some years after his arrival there, Edwards described his new hometown:

> The town of Northampton is about 82 years standing, and has about 200 families; which mostly dwell more compactly together than any town of such a bigness in these parts of the country. . . . Take the town in general, and so far as I can judge, they are as rational and understanding a people as most I have been acquainted with: many of them have been noted for religion, and particularly have been remarkable for their distinct knowledge in things that relate to heart religion and Christian experience, and their great regards thereto.[2]

Despite the strong communal spirit that had been forged by hardship and peril, work and worship, the town and even the church suffered a division based upon social inequality. While all the men were "freeholders," a few of the founding families were "proprietors," who held the reins of political power, social status, and personal wealth. Edwards later noted the town's central division:

> It has been a very great wound to the church of Northampton, that there has been for forty or fifty years, a sort of settled division of the people into two parties. . . . There have been some of the chief men in the town, of chief authority and wealth, that have been great proprietors of their lands, who have had one party with them. And the other party, which has commonly been the greatest, have been of those, who have been jealous of them, apt to envy them, and afraid of their having too much power and influence in town and church.[3]

As a result, the church at Northampton had suffered a series of "mighty contests and contentions" long before Edwards arrived there.

Notwithstanding this dissension, the church agreed "by a very great majority" to invite Edwards to "settle amongst them in the work of the ministry." This was November 1726. And on February 22, 1727, Edwards was ordained as "a Pastor of the Church of Northampton."

Edwards initially lived with his grandfather Solomon Stoddard, the longtime pastor. Stoddard had served the Northampton church for more than fifty years and was one of the most successful and influential preachers in all of New England. He was a serious student of the Scriptures, a widely read author, and a church and community leader. Stoddard's stature throughout the province was so great that he was dubbed the "Congregational Pope" of the Connecticut Valley.[4] Under his vibrant and searching preaching, Northampton experienced five separate seasons of revival, and the church grew from approximately one hundred communicants in 1677 to nearly five hundred communicant members in 1727, when Edwards arrived.

There is no doubt that Stoddard was a great man and a great minister. Yet his greatness was vitiated by a doctrinal peculiarity that would later haunt his grandson. It seems that although Stoddard answered the call to Northampton in 1669, he preached for two whole years without being formally ordained or even becoming a member of the church. Why? For the simple reason that he probably was not converted at the time; and if he were, he lacked assurance and any experiential knowledge of Christ. Then in April of 1672, while Stoddard was administering the Lord's Supper, Christ revealed himself to him.

As a result of his own conversion experience, Stoddard developed the erroneous notion that Communion, or the Lord's Supper, was a "converting ordinance," that "the place where the soul was likely to receive spiritual light and understanding was at the Lord's Table."[5] Previously it was assumed that to profess Christ included the profession of actually knowing Christ experientially; now, however, Stoddard proposed that if a person understood and professed a faith in the doctrines of Christianity and lived a morally upright life, then he should be permitted to partake of the Lord's Supper. Hopefully, the "half-way" Christian would find Christ in the ordinance. "It was better for the church and for the community, Stoddard came to argue, that the qualifications required for Communion should be as broad as possible."[6]

In effect, an individual with no experiential knowledge of Christ could partake of Communion and become a member of the visible church. Thus the sheepgate was opened to wolves. What Edwards thought of this practice when he joined Stoddard as his associate is uncertain. He did acquiesce in it for the time. What we do know, however, is that years later when he attempted to tighten the qualifications for Communion and membership, the wolves came out of hiding and attacked the shepherd.

Of course, the problems that would later grow out of the church's division and the pastor's doctrine were completely beyond Edwards' view. The distant thunder was hidden by the promising prospect of a long and fruitful ministry. He was young, idealistic, and hopeful. He was now in the vocation of his choice, where God had called him.

Moreover, only five months after taking his ministry vows, Edwards took his marriage vows. It seems that during his student days at Yale, Edwards had met Sarah Pierrepont, the daughter of James Pierrepont, one of the founders of Yale, and also a great-granddaughter of the famous Thomas Hooker, founder of Connecticut. She was a young woman with a reputation for uncommon godliness and beauty. Her parents provided her with a "polished education" and "the powers of her mind were of a superior order."[7] When Sarah was a budding young woman of only thirteen, and Edwards a twenty-year-old student at Yale, he grew enamored of her profound spirituality and wrote a glowing tribute on the flyleaf of his grammar book:

> They say there is a young lady in New Haven who is beloved of that almighty Being, who made and rules the world, and that there are certain seasons in which this great Being, in some way or other invisible, comes to her and fills her mind with exceeding sweet delight, and that she hardly cares for anything, except to meditate on him—that she expects after a while to be received up where he is, to be raised up

out of the world and caught up into heaven; being assured that he loves her too well to let her remain at a distance from him always. There she is to dwell with him, and to be ravished with his love and delight forever. Therefore if you present all the world before her, with the richest of its treasures, she disregards it and cares not for it, and is unmindful of any pain or affliction. She has a strange sweetness in her mind, and singular purity in her affections; is most just and conscientious in all her actions; and you could not persuade her to do anything wrong or sinful, if you would give her all the world, lest she should offend this great Being. She is of a wonderful sweetness, calmness and universal benevolence of mind; especially after those seasons in which this great God has manifested himself to her mind. She will sometimes go about from place to place, singing sweetly; and seems to be always full of joy and pleasure; and no one knows for what. She loves to be alone, and to wander in the fields and on the mountains, and seems to have someone invisible always conversing with her.[8]

Unfortunately, we have no record of how Jonathan and Sarah first met, or how their relationship blossomed into marriage. We do know, however, that only four years after penning this "Apostrophe," Jonathan and Sarah married, on July 28, 1727, in New Haven. The young newlyweds then returned to Northampton to establish a new home. The church had set the young minister's salary at one hundred pounds, with another three hundred set aside for the purchase of a homestead. In addition, Edwards received a total of fifty acres of land for pasture and farming. In little over a year, Sarah gave birth to their first daughter, and the young family was on its way to building a home and a church in Northampton.

4

Receiving the Mantle

I n February 1729 Solomon Stoddard passed away at
the ripe old age of eighty-one. The mantle now fell
on Edwards, and the full weight of ministerial re-
sponsibilities lay heavily upon his shoulders. Having
the duty of preaching three times a week, Edwards
rose early and studied hard—so hard, in fact, that in
the spring of 1729 he experienced a second breakdown
of his health. In order to recuperate, he spent the summer in New Haven, and then East Windsor. He returned to his ministry in late summer, and by all accounts the congregation was pleased with his
preaching. "The people of Northampton," his father
wrote at the time, "seem to have a great love and respect for him."[1]

It was Edwards' habit as a pastor to socialize little,
while studying and praying much. According to Samuel Hopkins, Edwards "commonly spent thirteen
hours, every day, in his study."[2] Sermon preparation
consumed a large part of his time. Like most young
preachers, Edwards struggled with the construction
of his sermons, striking out a word or phrase and re-
placing it with a better choice. Sermon construction
was hard work. Because he held a high view of the pul-

pit, he believed that it was his duty to thoroughly study the Scriptures and deliver to his congregation the mind of Christ:

> A minister by his office is to be the guide and instructor of his people. To that end he is to study and search the Scriptures and to teach the people, not the opinions of men—of other divines or of their ancestors—but the mind of Christ. As he is set to enlighten them, so a part of his duty is to rectify their mistakes, and, if he sees them out of the way of truth or duty, to be a voice behind them, saying, "This is the way, walk ye in it."[3]

In the early part of his ministry, Edwards usually wrote out his sermons in full. The form of his sermons was standard for the time: an exposition of a text, a doctrinal statement or thesis, a development section, and a closing application. When preaching, Edwards relied heavily on his notes. This was the practice he followed for about twenty years, or until the Great Awakening, at which time he began to preach from an outline or "skeleton." In contrast to the dramatic itinerant George Whitefield or the explosive orator Samuel Davies, Edwards' style was plain and simple. His voice was low and calm, he seldom used any gestures, and he frequently kept his eyes on his notes or on the bell rope at the back of the church. His great strength as a preacher, however, lay in his clear and forceful argumentation. His logical presentation of biblical truths was nearly irresistible. The listener's mind was overwhelmed, bowed down by the weight of truth. There was no escaping the force of Edwards' arguments. Moreover, he aimed the arrows of truth at the heart. He spoke in a pathetic manner, in the sense that he preached with a great depth of emotion or earnestness. For Edwards, subjects like heaven, hell, sin, and judgment were living realities, and his own sense of divine things was communicated to his audience. The real key to his success as a preacher, of course, was his intimacy with God. The Spirit of God dwelt in him and flowed through him as he preached.[4]

In addition to sermon preparation, Edwards spent many hours studying Scripture and theology. "Ministers should be diligent in their studies, and in the work of the ministry to which they are called," he said in a sermon on ministerial duty. "And particularly, ministers should be very conversant with the Holy Scriptures; making it very much their business, with the utmost diligence and strictness, to search those holy writings."[5] Edwards heeded his own advice. He studied constantly and then recorded his observations in general notebooks. These "Miscellanies" eventually equaled nine notebooks, in which he made regular entries from 1722 to the time of his death in 1758—over fourteen hundred entries in all. Every insight he thought worth remembering, he jotted in his notebooks. In fact, he was so addicted to penning his thoughts that when riding on horseback he would often pin a piece of paper to his jacket to recall a significant idea. By the time he arrived home, he looked as though he were covered with snowflakes. He would then hurry to his study, unpin the scraps, and duly record his insights.

The initial entries of the Miscellanies were chronologically lettered *a* through *z* (*j* and *v* were omitted). Then he used double letters (*aa, bb, . . . zz*), and soon after had to start a numerical system. For example:

> gg. *Religion. Purpose for Creation.* It is certain that God did not create the world for nothing. It is most certain that if there were no intelligent beings in the world, all the world would be without any good at all. . . . Wherefore, it necessarily follows that intelligent beings are the end of the creation, and that

their end must be to behold and admire the doings of God and magnify him for them, and to contemplate his glories in them. Wherefore, religion must be the end of the creation, the great end, the very end.

90. *Christian Religion: None Have Proved It False.* It is a convincing argument for the truth of the Christian religion, and that it stands upon a most sure basis, that none have ever yet been able to prove it false, though there have been many men of all sorts, many fine wits and men of great learning, that have spent themselves and ransacked the world for arguments against it, and this for many ages.[6]

Edwards never intended these notebooks to be published; nevertheless, they are a valuable resource for understanding his theology. His real goal was to store up useful material for his pulpit ministry. "While not directly related to sermon preparation, he saw the entries in his Miscellanies as an integral part of his life and thought both as a Christian and as a minister of the Word of God. . . . Study and writing were not ends in themselves. They were for the service of the gospel."[7]

Edwards understood that to be effective in the pulpit he needed to do more than simply master the mechanics of sermon preparation and the techniques of preaching. He also needed something beyond his solid knowledge of the Bible. What Edwards sought in private was communion with God. If he was going to preach effectively—with power—then he needed the touch of God. Not content to utter speculative truth alone, he strove to acquire a personal and experiential knowledge of the doctrines he proclaimed. He grasped the simple but profound fact that his inner life was interwoven with his outer work. Ministers should "earnestly seek after much of the spiritual knowledge of Christ, and that they may live in the clear views of his glory. . . . Ministers should be much in seeking God, and conversing with him by prayer, who is the fountain of light and love."[8]

Accordingly, Edwards spent much time in private prayer. He often kept days of fasting and prayer in secret; and he commonly spent hours on his knees in the prayerful reading of God's Word. His meditation, reading, and writing were all bathed in a spirit of prayer. His study became a holy sanctuary. His prayers were not perfunctory; he earnestly sought genuine, vital communion with God. The power he needed for the pulpit was the power of God.

Yet more fundamentally he sought after God because he loved God and yearned for His fellowship. Communion with Christ was his highest joy:

> I have sometimes had a sense of the excellent fullness of Christ, and his meetness and suitableness as a Savior; whereby he has appeared to me, far above all, the chief of ten thousands. And his blood and atonement has appeared sweet, and his righteousness sweet; which is always accompanied with an ardency of spirit, and inward strugglings and breathings and groanings, that cannot be uttered, to be emptied of myself, and swallowed up in Christ.[9]

The most important impact of Edwards' closet communion with Christ in the early years of his ministry was a growing sense of personal sinfulness. With God's beauty and holiness serving as a foil, he began to see his sin in a new light: indeed, in its true light—the light of God. He was humbled in the dust. Like the prophet Isaiah, gazing on the glory of the thrice holy God, he cried out, "Woe is me. I am a man of unclean lips!" Or like the patriarch Job, when confronted with God's sovereign majesty, he declared, "I have heard of thee by the hearing of the ear, but now mine eye seeth thee. Wherefore I abhor myself, and repent in dust and ashes." Edwards now realized "experientially," not just intellectually, the "exceeding sinfulness of sin."

> Often, since I have lived in this town, I have had very affecting views of my own sinfulness and vileness; very frequently to such a degree as to hold me in a kind of loud weeping, sometimes for a considerable time together; so that I have often been forced to shut myself up. I have had a vastly greater sense of my own wickedness, and the badness of my heart, than ever I had before my conversion. It has often appeared to me, that if God should mark iniquity against me, I should appear the very worst of all mankind; of all that have been since the beginning of the world to this time; and that I should have by far the lowest place in the world to this time; and that I should have by far the lowest place in hell. When others, that have come to talk with me about their soul concerns, have expressed the sense they have had of their own wickedness by saying, that it seemed to them, that they were as bad as the devil himself; I thought their expressions seemed exceeding faint and feeble, to represent my wickedness.
>
> My wickedness, as I am in myself, has long appeared to me perfectly ineffable, and swallowing up all thought and imagination; like an infinite deluge, or mountains over my head. I know not how to express better what my sins appear to me to be, than by heaping infinite upon infinite, and multiplying infinite by infinite. Very often, for these many years, these expressions are in my mind and in my mouth, "Infinite upon infinite—infinite upon infinite!" When I look into my heart, and take a view of my wickedness, it looks like an abyss, infinitely deeper than hell.[10]

Edwards' experiential knowledge of his own depravity led him to finally submit to, and then champion, the sovereignty of God. Peering into the abyss of his desperately wicked heart, he could fathom no way to salvation except God's free and sovereign grace.

> And it appears to me, that were it not for free grace, exalted and raised up to the infinite height of all the fullness and glory of the great Jehovah, and the arm of his power and grace stretched forth in all the majesty of his power, and in all the glory of his sovereignty, I should appear sunk down in my sins below hell itself; far beyond the sight of everything but the eye of sovereign grace, that can pierce even down to such a depth. And yet, it seems to me that my conviction of sin is exceeding small and faint; it is enough to amaze me, that I have very little sense of my sinfulness. I know certainly, that I have very little sense of my sinfulness. When I have had turns of weeping for my sins, I thought I knew at the time that my repentance was nothing to my sin.[11]

Since Edwards was the pastor of the most prominent church in western Massachusetts, he was asked to give the "Great and Thursday Lecture" in Boston on July 8, 1731. Reflecting his own spiritual experience, he chose as his text 1 Corinthians 1:29–31: "That no flesh should glory in his presence. But of him are ye in Christ Jesus, who of God is made unto us wisdom, and righteousness, and sanctification, and redemption: That, according as it is written, He that glorieth, let him glory in the Lord." The subject of the sermon was squarely stated: "That God is glorified in the work of redemption in this, that there appears in it so absolute and universal a dependence of the redeemed on him."

God Glorified in Man's Dependence, as the sermon was entitled, was Edwards' first publication. It was also a trumpet call to an apathetic ministry that was straying from the doctrines of the Puritan fathers. A growing number of ministers, such as Benjamin Wadsworth, the president of Harvard, were increasingly latitudinarian. And, while claiming to be orthodox Calvinists, they were reluctant to scruple over the "finer points" of doctrine. Edwards, on the other hand, courageously "stood before his elders, well aware of the 'enlightened' drift of things, and called them to the faith of their fathers, castigating 'schemes of divinity' that in any way mitigated the doctrine announced in his title."[12] As he said: "Hence those doctrines and schemes of divinity that are in any respect opposite to such an absolute and universal dependence on God, derogate from his glory, and thwart the design of our redemption."[13]

For the next two or three years Edwards' ministry proceeded normally. His private devotions were augmented by his voracious thirst for knowledge. With pen in hand, he read all the books he could acquire, especially books on divinity. His theology was predominantly Calvinistic, yet "he called no man father."[14] He inherited the Calvinism of his forefathers, yet he was a bold and original thinker who only accepted those doctrines that he believed were most harmonious with the Holy Scriptures. Of course, he studied his Bible above all. For Edwards, "the Bible was supreme: everything was subordinate to the Word of God."[15]

Edwards' pulpit ministry was apparently blessed, since his congregation asked him to publish one of his early (and now most famous) sermons. Entitled *A Divine and Supernatural Light Directly Imparted to the Soul*, Edwards was issuing a clarion call to personal conversion. Every individual, regardless of their relation to the visible church, needed to experience the new birth, or regeneration. God imparts to the soul supernatural light, or knowledge of Christ and divine things, and this knowledge is saving knowledge. Therefore, "this doctrine may well put us upon examining ourselves, whether we have ever had this divine light let into our souls."[16]

By 1734 there was a "great noise about Arminianism," wrote Edwards, "which seemed to appear with a very threatening aspect upon the interest of religion here."[17] In response, Edwards began to preach on the doctrinal issues in dispute. In a series of sermons collected as *Discourses on Various Important Subjects, Nearly Concerning the Great Affair of the Soul's Eternal Salvation*, Edwards reiterated and defended the traditional doctrine of justification by faith alone, as he had done earlier with the biblical teaching on regeneration.[18]

Several members of his extended family, most notably the Williamses, issued a strong statement to Edwards demanding that he "refrain from the controversy" and "not to publish his sentiments" regarding it. Edwards refused, and he was strongly criticized for entering the fray. His own cousin Israel Williams was of Arminian leanings and attacked him for defending orthodox Reformed theology. As Edwards said, "Great fault was found with 'meddling' with the controversy in the pulpit."[19]

Edwards' refusal to muzzle himself was, according to biographer Serono Dwight, "an offence not to be forgiven."[20] As we shall see, Israel Williams' lack of forgiveness would fester into a root of bitterness that would one day spring up and defile many.

5

Breaking Up the Fallow Ground

At the same time that Edwards was upholding the banner of Puritan orthodoxy, the Spirit of God, like a mighty rushing wind, swept into his Northampton church. And it was Edwards' opinion that the awakening in his church was directly related to biblical, orthodox preaching. The revival, he said, was "a remarkable testimony of God's approbation of the doctrine of *justification by faith alone.*" As he expounded this doctrine, many were led to question their standing with God and "to engage their hearts in a more earnest pursuit of justification."[1] The result was a general revival in Northampton and several surrounding towns.

In December of 1734 several people were "very suddenly" converted. And as the new year dawned a new interest in the things of Christ was evident throughout the town:

> A great and earnest concern about the great things of religion and the eternal world became universal in all parts of the town and among persons of all degrees and all ages. . . . Other discourse than of

the things of religion would scarcely be tolerated in any company.[2]

According to Edwards, the entire face of the town was wonderfully altered. The old pattern of backbiting and quarreling was put away, the taverns were left empty, family life was renewed, and every day resembled the Sabbath day. In addition, the townspeople now earnestly sought the "means of salvation, reading, prayer, meditation, the ordinances of God's house, and private conference. . . ." The universal cry was "What shall I do to be saved?"[3]

By the spring and summer of 1735 the town seemed full of God's presence: "There were remarkable tokens of God's presence in almost every house." One of the most notable evidences of revival was the spirit of public worship:

> Our public assemblies were beautiful: the congregation was alive in God's service, everyone earnestly intent on public worship, every hearer eager to drink in the words of the minister as they came from his mouth; the assembly in general was, from time to time, in tears while the word was preached; some weeping with sorrow and distress, others with joy and love, others with pity and concern for the souls of their neighbors.[4]

Many who had sat under the preaching of both Stoddard and Edwards received a new quickening from the Holy Spirit. The old story of the gospel took on a new beauty and power. Scales fell from their eyes. They beheld the wonders of the Cross and the beauties of the Savior. Edwards tells the story of an elderly woman who, having spent many years under Stoddard's powerful ministry, received new spiritual sight during the revival:

Reading in the New Testament concerning Christ's sufferings for sinners, she [was] astonished at what she read, at what was real and very wonderful but quite new to her. At first . . . she wondered within herself, that she had never heard of it before; but then immediately recollected herself, and thought she had often heard of it, and read it, but never till now saw it as real. She then cast in her mind how wonderful this was, that the Son of God should undergo such things for sinners, and how she had spent her time in ungratefully sinning against so good a God, and such a Saviour; though she was apparently a person of a very blameless and inoffensive life. And she was so overcome by these considerations that her nature was ready to fail under them: those who were about her, and knew not what was the matter, were surprised, and thought she was dying.[5]

Some whose eyes were suddenly opened broke forth into laughter, "tears often at the same time issuing like a flood, and intermingling a loud weeping." Others could not restrain themselves from "crying out with a loud voice, expressing their great admiration." At times some of the people were so overcome with such "longing desires after Christ" that their "natural strength" was taken from them. Their bodies were weakened, and they seemed to sink under the present sense of the excellency of Christ and the glory of God.[6]

Edwards was convinced that these conversions were genuine, not by the degree of emotional affection or intensity of physical manifestation, but by the godly fruit. First, the new converts had a profound humility. They in no way resembled the "assuming, self-conceited, and self-sufficient airs of enthusiasts." Instead, they exhibited a true spirit of meekness and desired to "lie low and in the dust before God." Indeed, they had no greater joy than when they were "lowest in the dust, emptied of themselves, and as it were annihilating themselves before God." Second, they had a love for God's written Word. "While God was so remarkably present amongst us by his Spirit, there was no book so delightful as the Bible. . . . There was no time so prized as the Lord's day, and no place in this world so desired as God's house." Third, there was a genuine love for the brethren and for the lost: "Our converts appeared remarkably united in dear affection for one another, and many have expressed much of that spirit of love which they have felt toward all mankind, and particularly to those who had been least friendly to them." Perhaps most significantly, Edwards argued that after the revival receded and the emotions abated, the fruit remained: "We still remain a reformed people, and God has evidently made us a new people." A few may have backslidden, "but in the main, there has been a great and marvellous work of conversion and sanctification among the people here."[7]

It is difficult to say exactly how many people were converted in Northampton during the revival of 1734–35, but Edwards suggests it was nearly three hundred. Of these, there were as many women as men, with the young, middle-aged, and elderly each visited by God. God is no respecter of persons.

In the midst of the general rejoicing, however, tragedy struck Edwards. His uncle, Joseph Hawley, committed suicide one Sabbath morning during the height of the revival. Some thought Hawley was driven to despair by the conviction of sin, and that, therefore, Edwards was at least partially responsible. What Hawley's two sons, Joseph Jr. and Elisha, thought of their father's death is unknown, but they continued to sit under Edwards' ministry and received his special care. In reality, Hawley was a victim of hereditary depression, his mother having died in the same way. He was not, as we shall see, the last Hawley hounded to self-destruction.

The revival placed new demands on Edwards. Public and private sermons were multiplied, prayer meetings were organized and attended, and personal visitation increased. The quickened townspeople, instead of loitering in the tavern for conversation, were now flocking to the parsonage for counseling. By the autumn of 1735 Edwards was exhausted, and his health again failed him. Since it was believed that horse riding built up one's physical constitution, Edwards took a journey to New York and New Jersey. During the trip he reestablished ties with several men who would later labor with him in the Great Awakening: Ebenezer Pemberton was now pastor of the Wall Street Church in New York, Jonathan Dickinson had settled in Elizabeth Town, and John Pierson was laboring in the parish at Woodbridge.

While visiting New Jersey, Edwards providentially met the Tennent brothers, who also were to play a major role in the upcoming revival. Their father, William Tennent, was a Presbyterian pastor and teacher at his "Log College," just north of Philadelphia. Each of his four sons, Gilbert, William Jr., John, and Charles, were preachers of "revitalized" Christianity. Although John died in 1732, the other brothers reported to Edwards that, like Northampton, each of their parishes had experienced recent awakenings. This was the first Edwards had heard of any revival outside of Northampton. He later learned that the revival touched many of the churches in the Connecticut Valley as well: South-Hadley, Deerfield, Hatfield, Enfield, East Windsor (his father's parish), Coventry, New Haven, and elsewhere.[8] Each of the men he visited had seen the power of God attend his ministry in the conversion of souls. Yet their desire for greater revival only intensified with their success.

When Edwards returned to Northampton, the congregation had voted (by a narrow margin) to construct a new meetinghouse. Work proceeded slowly throughout 1736. By June 1737 the spire was finished, and on December 25, 1737, the new building was occupied. Unfortunately, the building project was less than a harmonious effort; it led to a recurrence of Northampton's besetting sin of contention. In May of 1737 Edwards reproved the people for their contentious spirit: "I suppose for these thirty years people have not known how to manage scarcely any public business without dividing into parties. Of late, time after time, that old party spirit has appeared again, and particularly this spring."[9]

Edwards realized that although the work of the recent revival was real, it was not necessarily deep. Conversion is not consecration. These new converts might be genuinely saved, but now they needed to be genuinely sanctified. Thus he spent the next two years preaching on holiness and Christian growth. In both *Charity and Its Fruits* (1738) and *A History of the Work of Redemption* (1739) he drove home the message dear to his own heart: "He that truly loves God, constantly seeks after God in the course of his life: seeks his grace, and acceptance, and glory." In light of God's gracious visitation of Northampton, with the many conversions that resulted, Edwards pleaded with his people to respond with a "holy, serious, just, humble, charitable" devotion of themselves to God and to one another.[10]

Increased demands on Edwards' time notwithstanding, he did not neglect his wife and family. He daily met with Sarah in his study for prayer and encouragement, as well as planning family business. Many of the daily concerns of the household, such as organizing chores, buying food, and governing the children, were placed in her hands. By 1738 Edwards had six children. Daughter Sarah was born in 1728, and the rest followed every two years: Jerusha (1730), Esther (1732), Mary (1734), Lucy (1736), and Timothy (1738). It was Edwards' habit to conduct family prayers both in the morning and before bedtime. Often he would take one of his children into his study and address him concerning his (or her) spiritual condition. He also taught his children spiritual truth by catechizing them in the Westminster Shorter Catechism on the evening before every Sabbath.

In the meantime, word of the "frontier" revival was spreading. There was a great deal of interest and not a little skepticism concerning the reports of Northampton. Responding to questions from Benjamin Coleman, a prominent Boston pastor, Edwards had earlier (May 1735) given a written report of the awakening. Coleman, in turn, had passed on Edwards' reply to two English divines, John Guyse and Isaac Watts, who wrote back to Coleman asking for a more detailed report. Edwards complied with their request and dispatched a long letter (November 6, 1736) in which he estimates the number of converts at Northampton and also mentions that the revival was occurring in isolated churches throughout New England. Elisha Williams had also written to Watts in May of 1736, stating that "there has been a remarkable revival of religion in several parts of this country, in ten parishes in the county of Hampshire, in the Massachusetts province, where it first began a little more than a year since, and in near twenty parishes of this colony [Connecticut]."[11]

When Guyse and Watts received Edwards' full letter, they were so impressed with the glorious report that they immediately determined to publish it. "So strange and surprising a work of God that we have not heard anything like it since the Reformation . . . should be published and left upon record," they wrote to Coleman. Eventually, in the autumn of 1737, Edwards' long letter was published in London with the lengthy title *A Faithful Narrative of the Surprising Work of God in the Conversion of Many Souls in Northampton and Neighboring Towns and Villages of New Hampshire in New England.*[12]

This little book with a long title became, through God's providence, one of the most popular and influential books of its day. In only two years *Faithful Narrative* went through three editions and twenty printings and reached the far corners of the Colonies and Britain. "Far away in Boston, and farther still in England and Scotland, prominent theologians and ministers were thrilled by the news and convinced that a new day of the Lord was at hand."[13] John Wesley, for instance, noted in his *Journal*: "I set out for Oxford. In walking, I read the truly surprising narrative of the conversions lately wrought in and about the town of Northampton, in New England. Surely 'this is the Lord's doing, and it is marvellous in our eyes.' "[14] Reading about the works of God in Northampton, Wesley and others were inspired to believe that God could in their own day bring in a mighty harvest of souls. They were, in effect, led to desire and pray for a great awakening.

6

The Great Awakening

The grand revival known as the "Great Awakening" was a phenomenon that shook the English-speaking world during the late 1730s and 1740s. The flames of revival that scorched the American Colonies were likewise ablaze in England, Scotland, and Ireland. Yet the very notion of revival supposes a previous state of decline, or at least complacency, in religious and spiritual matters. If the late '30s and '40s was a time of revival, what conditions characterized the state of Western religion before this time?

In England, deism had the upper hand in religious circles. As an expression of religious rationalism, deism advocated that God was little more than a first cause, a force that made the world the way a clockmaker designs a clock. Then, having set the mechanism in motion, He simply allowed it to run according to natural laws. This deity, therefore, did not interfere with His own laws; thus miraculous intervention by God was excluded. Under the name of "Natural Religion," authors such as Matthew Tindal, John Toland, and Thomas Woolston claimed that deism was true primitive Christianity.

Of course, deism did not go unchallenged by the established church: Bishop Butler wrote his masterful apologetic *The Analogy of Revealed Religion*, and William Law penned *An Appeal to All That Doubt the Truths of Revelation*. The famous hymnist Isaac Watts, who took an avid interest in the revival in Northampton, also wielded his sword in the Trinitarian Controversy when he issued his sublime *A Treatise on the Trinity*. Nevertheless, British Christianity proved itself to be little more than a sedate and timid religious ethic unable to resist the decay of spirituality and morality. Mourning the lack of spiritual power among both the clergy and the people, Rev. Howe noted,

> It is plain, too sadly plain, there is a great retraction of the Spirit of God even from us [ministers]. We know not how to speak living sense unto souls; how to get within you: our words die in our mouths, or drop and die between you and us. We even faint when we speak; long-experienced unsuccessfulness makes us despond: we speak not as persons that hope to prevail, that expect to make you serious, heavenly, mindful of God, and to walk more like Christians.[1]

In the midst of this deistical decline in religion, George Whitefield was brought into the world. Since he played such a large role in the Great Awakening, a few words about his history are in order. Born in December 1714, Whitefield entered college at the age of eighteen, and met the Wesley brothers a year later. He was ordained at the age of twenty-one on Trinity Sunday, 1736. Shortly thereafter, he was invited to minister in London, and while there he first received letters from friends in Georgia, bidding him to come to the Colony and help them. After being detained sometime in London, Whitefield left England in January of 1738 and arrived in Savannah in May of the same year. While there, he observed the deplorable conditions of some orphan children; and, possibly at the suggestion of Charles Wesley, he designed to build an orphanage. In order to raise funds, he decided to return to England. This he did, arriving at London in early December.

A week later Whitefield preached twice and solicited funds for his orphanage. Within a matter of days, however, the established clergy took issue with his doctrine of regeneration and viciously attacked him from pulpit and press. Having the church doors slammed in his face, so to speak, Whitefield marched to the fields. On Wednesday, February 21, he preached his first open-air sermon at Kingswood, with nearly two thousand in attendance. On Friday he preached to about four or five thousand and on Sunday to approximately ten thousand. The Great Awakening had erupted!

But Whitefield had not forgotten his orphans. His goal was to return to Savannah and build them a home. So he entrusted the blossoming revival in England to the Wesleys and sailed to the Colonies.

At the time of his arrival on October 30, 1739, a number of locations (Northampton among them) were already experiencing revival of their own. Previous to 1720, however, the spiritual and religious conditions were little better than in England. Due to the influence of the Half-Way Covenant and Stoddard's doctrine of the Lord's Supper, many unconverted people became members of the visible church. Worse still, many unconverted men began to enter the ministry. Thus "the difference between the church and the world was vanishing away. Church discipline was neglected, and the growing laxness of morals was invading the churches."[2]

In the 1720s things began to change, however. For the next fifteen years evangelical revivals were experienced in different parts of the Colonies. In Pennsylvania, for instance, the German people of many denominations—Lutheran, Mennonite, Quaker—had settled northwest of Philadelphia in a community named Germantown. During this period the old pietistic influences were rekindled, especially among the Mennonites and Baptists. In New Jersey, the ministry of Theodorus Frelinghuysen, a Dutch Reformed minister, began to bear fruit in the country of the Raritan Valley. In the Middle Colonies, the Presbyterians also started to experience awakenings through the efforts of William Tennent and his sons. And in New England, of course, was Edwards. So by the time Whitefield arrived in Pennsylvania in 1739, the Colonial soil had been ploughed and was awaiting the sower and his seed.

Whitefield made four tours of the Colonies in the years 1738 to 1740. The first, or the winter tour, began in Pennsylvania in November 1739 and covered New Jersey, New York, Maryland, Virginia, and North and South Carolina. During this tour Whitefield made two important acquaintances: Gilbert Tennent and Benjamin Franklin—the latter becoming his publisher in America. In January the tour ended at Savannah, the site where the orphanage was to be built.

The spring tour, which began in April of 1740, again took Whitefield to Philadelphia and New York. After four and a half weeks of travel, he again returned to Georgia on June 5, "having accomplished the purposes for which he had taken the tour, for not only had he been mightily used of God in the reviving of the work in the Middle Colonies, but had collected about 500 pounds with which to continue the House of Mercy in Georgia."[3]

The summer tour, which lasted the greater part of July 1740, and covered Charlestown, Massachusetts, and the surrounding area, was fruitful, although it was marked by tremendous opposition from Bishop Gardner of Charlestown.

Whitefield's final and most extensive tour was in the autumn of 1740. Having arrived in Rhode Island on Sunday, September 14, he spent the following four months traveling throughout New England. Not only did he have the pleasure of meeting with Edwards in Northampton, he also had the honor of preaching from his pulpit. Moreover, during the autumn tour, Whitefield had a great influence on the Honorable Jonathan Belcher, the governor of Massachusetts. In 1745 Belcher became governor of New Jersey, and in 1746 he played a key role in the establishment of a new Presbyterian theological school, Princeton College.

The effect of Whitefield's preaching was nothing short of dramatic. An anonymous letter to the *New England Journal* stated:

> I went to hear him in the evening at the Presbyterian Church. . . . I never in my life saw so attentive an audience. Mr. Whitefield spoke as one having authority: all he said was Demonstration, Life and Power. The people's eyes and ears hung on his lips. They greedily devoured every word. I came home astonished. Every scruple vanished; I never saw or heard the like; and I said within myself, Surely God is with this man of a truth![4]

When Whitefield was in Philadelphia, Benjamin Franklin came to hear him preach and gave striking testimony to his persuasive powers. In reference to Whitefield's pleading for his orphans, Franklin said,

> Mr. Whitefield . . . preached up this charity, and made large collections, for his eloquence had a won-

derful power over the hearts and purses of his hearers, of which I myself was an instance.

I happened . . . to attend one of his sermons, in the course of which I perceived he intended to finish with a collection, and I silently resolved he should get nothing from me. I had in my pocket a handful of copper money, three or four silver dollars, and five pistoles in gold. As he proceeded I began to soften, and concluded to give the coppers. Another stroke of his oratory made me ashamed of that, and determined me to give the silver; and he finished so admirably that I emptied my pocket wholly into the collector's dish, gold and all.[5]

Everywhere Whitefield went his preaching had a powerful impact. His *Journals* records that "many men melted into tears" and that after the preaching, many began to press upon him in his private hours. On Thursday, April 17, during the spring tour, he states that he "preached to upwards of ten thousand people. . . . Hundreds were graciously melted. . . ." Two days later he records "giving answers and praying with diverse persons who applied to me under deep convictions."[6] In summing up the spring tour, he declared, "Religion is all the talk; and I think I can say the Lord Jesus hath gotten Himself the victory in many hearts."[7]

By the time Whitefield arrived at Northampton in 1740, the revival had already been underway for months. According to Edwards, in the spring of that year there was a "visible alteration" in the town. People were more serious and religious in their conversation, and many people began to consult Edwards concerning their spiritual condition.

On October 17 Whitefield crossed the ferry to Northampton, and in the space of three days preached four sermons at the church and one at Edwards' home.

Referring to the church services, Whitefield wrote: "Preached this morning and good Mr. Edwards wept during the whole time of exercise. The people were equally affected; and in the afternoon the power increased yet more. I have not seen four such gracious meetings together since my arrival."[8] Edwards concurred: "The congregation was extraordinarily melted by every sermon; almost the whole assembly being in tears for a great part of the sermon time."[9]

Edwards and his guest then set out for East Windsor, where Whitefield preached on October 21. The next day the two parted company: Edwards headed up to Connecticut, and Whitefield finished up his tour of New England. In the meantime, the revival in Northampton increased throughout 1740. Edwards noted:

> The revival at first appeared chiefly among professors and those that had entertained hope that they were in a state of salvation, to whom Mr. Whitefield chiefly addressed himself; but in a very short time there appeared an awakening and deep concern among some young persons that looked upon themselves in a Christless state; and there were some hopeful appearances of conversion, and some professors were greatly revived. In about a month or six weeks, there was a great attention in the town, both as to the revival of professors and the awakening of others.[10]

The revival gathered steam during the last part of the year with a powerful work occurring among Northampton's young people. By December "religious subjects almost wholly took up the conversation" of the town's youth.

The quickening spread during the winter and into spring. In May of 1741 Edwards preached in a private house, and toward the end of his message several people were so overcome with the "glory of divine things" that there was "a very visible effect upon their bodies." The young people present were quickly moved into another room and, after a short time of discussion with Edwards, were "overcome with distress" about their sinful condition. The room filled with "outcries, faintings, and the like." The awakening of the young was so extensive that Edwards thereafter set up special meetings for them in which he would give "counsels proper to their age." It was not uncommon at these meetings for the room to be "filled with cries," and when the children were dismissed, "they almost all of them went home crying aloud through the streets. . . ."[11]

As the Great Awakening gained momentum, Edwards was often called upon to preach at churches outside of Northampton. In July 1741, for instance, Edwards and Eleazer Wheelock went to Enfield, where Edwards gave his famous sermon "Sinners in the Hands of an Angry God."

Wheelock thought the people of Enfield were "loose and vain," not having been touched by the revival. On the evening of July 8, at an unannounced lecture, Edwards entered the pulpit and declared his text, Deuteronomy 32:35: "Their foot shall slide in due time." His doctrine, he warned the congregation, was that "there is nothing that keeps wicked men at any one moment out of hell, but the mere pleasure of God." There is no lack of power in God to send every sinner to hell immediately if He should choose to do so. Indeed, since wicked men justly deserve damnation, and even now are under God's righteous wrath, nothing but God's mere pleasure keeps them from descending into hell at any given instant. God's arm is not shortened. Thus there is no security for the wicked. God can take sinners out of this world in countless ways. "Unconverted men walk over the pit of hell on a rotten covering, and there are innumerable places in this covering so weak that they won't bear their weight, and these places are not seen. The arrows of death fly unseen at noonday; the sharpest sight can't discern them." The dreadful reality of unregenerate men is that they "are held in the hand of God over the pit of hell; they deserved the fiery pit, and are already sentenced to it. . . . The devil is waiting for them, hell is gaping for them, the flames gather and flash about them, and would fain lay hold on them, and swallow them up. . . ." Only the "mere arbitrary will" of an incensed God keeps them from eternal destruction.

With a holy zeal in his eyes, Edwards bore down on the carnally secure. "The bow of God's wrath is bent, and the arrow made ready on the string, and justice bends the arrow at your heart, and strains the bow, and it is nothing but the mere pleasure of God, and that of an angry God . . . that keeps the arrow one moment from being made drunk with your blood." Do not be deceived by false cries of "peace and safety." Your condition is as precarious as a spider hung over a fire. "The God that holds you over the pit of hell, much as one holds a spider, or some loathsome insect, over the fire, abhors you, and is dreadfully provoked; his wrath towards you burns like fire; he looks upon you as worthy of nothing else, but to be cast into the fire. . . ." Edwards then pleaded with his audience to ponder their perilous exposure to punishment:

> O Sinners! Consider the fearful danger you are in: 'tis a great furnace of wrath, a wide and bottomless pit, full of the fire of wrath, that you are held over in the hand of that God whose wrath is provoked and incensed as much against you as against any of the damned in hell: you hang by a slender thread, with the flames of divine wrath flashing about it, and

ready every moment to singe it, and burn it asunder; and you have no interest in any mediator, and nothing to lay hold of to save yourself, nothing to keep off the flames of wrath, nothing of your own, nothing that you ever have done, nothing that you can do, to induce God to spare you one moment.[12]

As the horrible reality set in, there was a great groaning throughout the meetingplace. Numbers began to shriek and cry out, "What shall I do to be saved?" Others howled: "Oh, I am going to hell!"[13] Some clung to their seats for fear of falling at that very moment into the burning lake of fire. Edwards paused and tried to restrain the groans and weeping. He then continued, "Now God stands ready to pity you; this is a day of mercy; you may cry now with some encouragement of obtaining mercy: but when once the day of mercy is past, your most lamentable and dolorous cries and shrieks will be in vain." Echoing the words of the angels at Sodom, Edwards admonished all to flee from the wrath to come: "Haste and escape for your lives, look not behind you, escape to the mountain, lest you be consumed."[14]

Wheelock, observing the scene, said the people were "bowed down with an awful conviction of their sin and danger." After Edwards descended from the pulpit, the people were gathered into groups for prayer. Many were changed. As another eyewitness recorded: "Several souls were hopefully wrought upon that night, and oh the cheerfulness and pleasantness of their countenances that received comfort."[15]

Incidents like this were common throughout the Great Awakening. In fact, manifestations such as jerking, fainting, and crying out occurred frequently during the spring and summer of 1741 in Northampton. Edwards commented, "It was a very frequent thing to see a house full of outcries, faintings, convulsions, and such like, both with distress, and also with admiration and joy." In some cases, individuals were "so affected, and their bodies so overcome, that they could not go home, but were obliged to stay all night where they were."[16]

As might be expected, these extreme manifestations caused some onlookers to doubt the authenticity of the revival. Did an extraordinary show of affection signal an exceptional work of grace? Was this God, the devil, or the flesh? How could one tell?

Similar questions were on many minds when Edwards was asked to give the commencement sermon at Yale in September 1741. His message, entitled "The Distinguishing Marks of a Work of the Spirit of God," was Edwards' answer to these questions. He chose as his text 1 John 4:1: "Beloved, believe not every spirit, but try the spirits whether they are of God: because many false prophets are gone out into the world." In a highly rational but not dispassionate presentation, Edwards argued that the Great Awakening should not be discounted because of the extreme physical manifestations such as "tears, trembling, groans, loud outcries, agonies of body, or the failing of bodily strength." On the other hand, neither do these physical symptoms prove that the work is truly of God:

> A work is not to be judged by any effects on the bodies of men; such as tears, trembling, groans, loud outcries, agonies of body, or the failing of bodily strength. The influence persons are under is not to be judged one way or other by such effects on the body; and the reason is because the Scripture nowhere gives us any such rule.[17]

So how do we judge? We "try the spirits" or judge a particular work by the rules set forth in the written Word of God. That is the standard by which we judge all subjective experience or physical manifestations. And according to Edwards, there were five "distinguishing marks" of a true work of God's Spirit:

> The Holy Spirit always (1) engenders a greater esteem for Jesus; (2) operates against the kingdom of Satan; (3) causes men to have a greater regard for the Holy Scriptures; (4) leads people into truth; and (5) operates as a spirit of love to God and man. If these marks are present, despite irregularities, then one can be sure that the Spirit of God is at work.[18]

Edwards realized that the awakening was tainted in some cases by fanaticism and error. These "stumbling blocks," as he called them, were not likely to be removed; rather, they might even increase. Yet instead of sitting back as cool spectators, he felt it was the duty of all Christians, and especially Christian ministers, to do all in their power to promote the revival. Edwards then issued this strong admonition: "Let us all be warned, by no means to oppose, or do anything in the least to clog or hinder the work; but, on the contrary, do our utmost to promote it."[19]

By publishing this sermon, Edwards became the awakening's leading proponent. He was also now marked as New England's principal apologist of experiential religion.

7

Apologist of Experiential Religion

The awakening continued unabated during the winter of 1741–42. And for his own part, Edwards was doing his utmost to promote the revival. Besides his labors at Northampton, he frequently journeyed to preach in other parishes, while leaving his pulpit in the hands of visiting ministers. On one such occasion, in late January of 1742, Edwards traveled to Leicester on a missionary tour and turned his pulpit over to a Mr. Buell. Under Buell's preaching, the excitement in Northampton reached a feverish pitch. Services were conducted nearly every night for two weeks, and when outside the pulpit, Buell was kept extremely busy in private ministry.

Around this time Sarah Edwards experienced a marvelous quickening from God: "I felt more perfectly subdued and weaned from the world," she later wrote, "than I had ever been conscious of before. . . . I was entirely swallowed up in God, as my only portion, and his honour and glory was the object of my supreme delight." Throughout the night of January 28 Sarah tasted the blessedness of her dear Savior: "All night I continued in a constant, clear, and lively sense of the heavenly sweetness of Christ's excellent and transcendent love. . . ." This constant calmness of soul was like a "flowing and reflowing of heavenly and divine love, from Christ's heart to mine. . . ." There was no earthly pleasure that could compare to the "pure delight which fed and satisfied the soul. . . ." It was "a sweetness which my soul was lost in. It seemed to be all that my feeble frame could sustain of that fullness of joy which is felt by those who behold the face of Christ and share his love in the heavenly world."[1]

Sarah's experience speaks of all that was good in the revival. But a darker expression of the awakening was beginning to surface in Northampton. When Edwards returned home he found the town in "a great and continual commotion" and in "very extraordinary circumstances." New, suspicious manifestations were emerging: "There were some instances of persons lying in a sort of trance, remaining perhaps for a whole twenty-four hours motionless, and with their senses locked up; but in the meantime under strong imaginations, as though they went to heaven and had there a vision of glorious and delightful objects."[2]

What did Edwards think of these extreme displays? He denounced them in no uncertain terms. They were instigated by the devil. "When the people were raised to this height, Satan took the advantage. . . ."[3] Edwards noted that the early part of the revival had been very pure, "having less of a corrupt mixture than in the former great outpouring of the Spirit in 1735 and 1736." Yet in the latter part of the Great Awakening (1742), his people were "infected from abroad"—by which he probably meant Buell and some of his devotees who had followed him from Suffield to Northampton. Their "raptures," violent emotions, and vehement zeal beguiled some of Edwards' flock into imagining they were superior in grace. This was a "strange influence," thought Edwards. And he labored with difficulty to deliver some from their delusion.[4]

Reflecting later on events in Northampton, Edwards was convinced more than ever of the need to "try the spirits." Physical manifestations alone tell us nothing about the nature of a person's spiritual experience. Extreme emotions or bodily manifestations, in and of themselves, are not a sure sign of God's gracious work. Rather, the spirit must be judged by its long-term fruit. It is not enough for the emotions to be elevated or the body agitated; the soul itself must be touched and transformed. As Edwards put it, we must look to "the temper of the soul," not only at the time of quickening but "remaining afterwards."[5] Or, as Christ himself said, "By their fruits ye shall know them."

Indeed, if there was ever a time when discernment yielded a premium, it was during the latter days of the Great Awakening. As it turned out, the same aberrations happening at Northampton were transpiring elsewhere, among both the laity and the clergy.

One of the most notorious examples of "enthusiasm," as it was called, was the Rev. James Davenport, the "archfanatic" of the Great Awakening.[6] Davenport was born at Stamford, Connecticut, a great-grandson of New Haven's founder, John Davenport, and a graduate of Yale. Since 1738 he was pastor of the old Puritan church at Southold on Long Island. Being much impressed with the itinerant ministry of Whitefield and Tennent, Davenport fancied he was called to imitate them. Claiming that he had received a word from God to "go into the Philistine's camp," he deserted his church and began to travel to other churches un-invited. Under his preaching there probably were a number of conversions; however, there was also an in-crease of bizarre manifestations: jerkings, faintings, and trances. In fact, he even encouraged such behav-ior by his own eccentricity. One eyewitness wrote:

> He has no knack at raising the Passions, but by a violent straining of his Lungs, and the most extrav-agant writhings of his Body, which at the same Time that it creates Laughter and Indignation in the most, occasions great meltings, screamings, crying, swoon-ing, and Fits in some others. . . . Were you to see him in his most violent agitations, you would be apt to think, that he was a Madman just broke from his Chains: But especially had you seen him returning from the Common Way thro' the Streets, he with his Hands extended, his Head thrown back, and his Eyes staring up to Heaven, attended with so much Dis-order, that they look'd more like a Company of Bac-chanalians after a mad Frolick, than sober Christians who had been worshipping God. . . .[7]

Davenport would often show up at a church un-invited, demand the pulpit, and, if refused, denounce the minister as unconverted. His fanatical harangues against the clergy aroused resentment everywhere he went. And since he thought most ministers uncon-verted, he exhorted their flocks to desert them. Thus he was a major source of heated alienation and bitter division.

It is not surprising, then, that both the civil and ecclesiastical authorities banded together to resist him. In 1742 he was arrested in Connecticut for vio-lating the law against itinerant preaching, adjudged mentally disturbed, and deported to Long Island. Now that he was filled with the "spirit of martyrdom," Dav-enport headed for Boston, where he again filled the streets with denunciatory preaching and extravagant claims of divine "impressions." A convention of ministers there denounced Davenport for his "errors, irregularities, and mischiefs," and warned the people that he was "deeply tinctured with a spirit of enthusiasm."[8] A few weeks later he was arrested, declared *non compos mentis* (not of sound mind), and expelled.

Davenport's fanatical finale took place in March 1743, when he gathered a group of zealots in New London to start a new church. In response to divine dreams, he told his followers that they needed to purify themselves from worldliness; accordingly, "he ordered wigs, cloaks and breeches, hoods, gowns, rings, jewels and necklaces to be brought together into his room, and laid in a heap, that they might, by his solemn decree, be committed to the flames."[9] He next issued a list of books that likewise needed to be burned—evangelical heroes such as John Flavel, William Beveridge, Increase Mather, and others. On March 6 Davenport and his followers marched to the wharf and in a frenzied ceremony burned the collected articles while shouting "Hallelujah!" and "Glory to God!"[10]

The outlandish behavior of Davenport and others gave ammunition to the enemies of the awakening. As early as January 1742 an anonymous author published a letter titled "The Wonderful Narrative," which was a pseudo-history of the "French Prophets, Their Agitations, Extasies and Imaginations." The design of the author (probably Charles Chauncy, junior pastor of Boston's First Church) was to blacken the revival with the label of "fanaticism." Chauncy's intention was to discredit the revival by showing that such actions as fainting or outcries were not signs of the Holy Spirit but the work of enthusiasm or even imposture, as was the case with the French prophets.

Next, in August of the same year, another letter (again probably by Chauncy) appeared in which the writer vilified the ministry of Whitefield: "I freely acknowledge, wherever he went he generally moved the passions, especially of the younger people, and the females among them. . . . But so far as I could judge . . . the town, in general, was not mended in those things wherein a reformation is greatly needed." This testimony, though, was directly contradicted by a statement of Benjamin Franklin, hardly a "friend" of the revival. And Chauncy continued his letter with a direct denunciation of the revival as nothing more than a "Spirit of Superstition and Enthusiasm reigning in the Land."[11]

Edwards entered the fray in March 1743 (providentially the same month that Davenport conducted his flaming farewell service) by publishing *Some Thoughts Concerning the Present Revival.* Chauncy's reply, *Seasonable Thoughts on the State of Religion in New England,* was circulating six months later. It was clear that the battle lines were now distinctly drawn, with the troops gathering around Edwards and Chauncy as their opposing generals.

Chauncy's position was that the "revival" (if it could be called that) may have done some good, but on the whole there was more evil than good, and therefore the "commotion" should stop. In particular, Chauncy and other anti-revivalists criticized not only the bodily manifestations apparent in the revival but also itinerant preaching, lay exhorting, censoriousness, church separations, and other miscellaneous doctrinal errors, such as the belief in direct divine impressions.

In *Some Thoughts,* Edwards had to walk a tightrope: He had to defend the revival from its critics, but also guard the revival from its friends. (With friends like Davenport, who needed enemies!)

Edwards believed that, in the main, the revival was a veritable work of God's Spirit. This is apparent from the amount of space he gives to defending and promoting the revival. In fact, in the early Edinburgh edition of *Some Thoughts* (1743), Edwards devotes fifty pages to arguing that the revival is indeed "a glorious work of God." He then devotes section two of the work to exhorting all to "acknowledge this work" (24 pages), and section three provides advice for "what ought to be done to promote this work" (31 pages). Clearly Edwards thought the revival was genuine and deserved the active support of all Christians.[12]

Nevertheless, he now realized more than ever that the revival had been infected with carnal enthusiasm and demonic influence. Therefore, he devoted the largest section of *Some Thoughts* to "things to be corrected and avoided." Here he addressed the "friends" of the revival who, through errors and extremes, were bringing the revival into disfavor. In agreement with the antirevivalists, Edwards castigated fanatics for spiritual pride, for denouncing ministers, for separating from their churches, for following immediate revelations, and for other faults.[13] Despite these defects, Edwards still maintained that the awakening was a true work of God.

Meanwhile, as *Some Thoughts* was circulating throughout Great Britain and the Colonies, Edwards was back in Northampton managing the awakening there. Perhaps in response to some of the excesses, he decided to lead his people in a solemn public covenant with God. On March 16, 1742, the people of God at Northampton swore: "We do this day present ourselves before the Lord, to renounce our evil ways; we put away our abominations from before God's eyes, and with one accord, to renew our engagements to seek and serve God. . . ." As the covenant stipulated, the people promised to observe the rules of honesty, justice, and uprightness; to not injure one's neighbor; to provide restitution for past wrongs; to refrain from backbiting and strife; to not violate justice for private gain; to not indulge ill will or hold secret grudges; to do nothing that might gratify lust and hinder the spirit of religion; and to fulfill all the relative duties of parents, spouses, and children. Finally, the people promised "to be often strictly examining ourselves by these promises, especially before the sacrament of the Lord's Supper; and beg of God that he would, for Christ's sake, keep us from wickedly dissembling in these our solemn vows. . . ."[14]

This covenant was essentially a formal expression of Edwards' belief about real spiritual experience: it must always produce a greater dedication to God and man. In a way, the public covenant was a test for all those in his church who believed they had been quickened during the revival. Would they step forward and publicly dedicate themselves to God?

Edwards also took further steps to see that his flock understood the true nature of saving and sanctifying grace. Throughout late 1742 and 1743 he preached a series of sermons on 1 Peter 1:18, which were later published (1746) as *A Treatise Concerning the Religious Affections*. Today hailed as a masterpiece of "religious psychology," *Religious Affections* was Edwards' attempt to get at the root issue in the controversy over the Great Awakening: namely, what is the nature of true conversion? Or as Edwards put it: "What is the nature of true religion? And wherein do lie the distinguishing notes of that virtue and holiness that is acceptable in the sight of God?"[15]

In order to answer this question, Edwards first admits that the recent revival contained a "mixture of counterfeit religion with true" and that "the devil has had his greatest advantage against the cause and kingdom of Christ all along hitherto." It was precisely because this mixture had caused such confusion that Edwards felt the need to address the issue.

In summary, Edwards begins by discriminating between "false and gracious affections," and also between affections and "passions." The latter are dark emotions that actually hinder the formation of "gracious affections." Edwards then identified love as the controlling affection. Throughout this section he demonstrates from the Scriptures the large part that affections played in the life of eminent saints.

In the second part Edwards describes those signs that indicate false affections. Or, to put it differently, he here argues that certain "signs," such as bodily effects, fervor, zeal, praise, moving testimonies, and others, do not necessarily prove a genuine work of the Spirit. Edwards was strongly skeptical that a mere religious activity such as reading, praying, or singing was a sign of true godly affection. By themselves, these "signs" are no guarantee of saving grace.

In the third and largest part of his *Religious Affections*, Edwards gives a detailed description of twelve signs of "truly gracious and holy affections." They are:

    I. Gracious Affections are from Divine Influence
   II. Their Object is the Excellence of Divine Things
  III. They are founded on the moral Excellency of Objects
  IV. They arise from Divine Illumination

While space does not permit a thorough analysis of these signs, it is important to note a few features of Edwards' exposition. First of all, he avoids the false dichotomy between "head and heart." The affections are not emotions; rather, they are inclinations of the will in response to the mind. Although the emotions are involved, true religious affections are rooted in a divinely enlightened mind. Thus he was definitely not advocating "emotionalism" as we use that term today.

Second, Edwards is clearly distancing himself from the fanatical fringe of the Great Awakening. He does this by pointing out that true religion reveals itself in virtues such as "evangelical humiliation" and "the temper of Jesus." Nothing was more repugnant to Edwards than the pride and arrogance of enthusiasts like Davenport. What is missing from their experience is humility, a sense of sin, and true repentance. "All gracious affections are broken-hearted affections," he argued.[16] And true saints are "those that do mourn" for their sins.[17]

Third, it is obvious from Edwards' treatment of the affections that he believed the crucial test of any spiritual experience was a life of holiness. When the Holy

Spirit abides in the soul, He imparts to it His own special property of holiness. A true convert, therefore, will demonstrate a permanent change of temper. He will now be inclined away from evil and toward good. For a true saint, holiness is "the most amiable and sweet thing that is to be found in heaven or earth."[18] He will be grieved at his remaining corruption and strive after holiness. He will resolve to live a life of obedience to God. That is perhaps the most important point to be made on the subject. Over and over again, Edwards hammers away at the fallacy of cheap grace. Affections are an important part of true religion; but if the life is not changed—and changed in the direction of holiness—then the affections are false and the religion is vain.

Finally, Edwards never intended to establish a "checklist" with which to judge the spiritual state of others. On the contrary, the purpose of the *Religious Affections* was to aid converts of the revival in evaluating their own condition. These "signs" were not infallible marks for separating the sheep from the goats, for only God truly knows the hearts of men. He put it like this:

> Though it is plain that Christ has given rules to all Christians to enable them to judge professors of religion whom they are concerned with, so far as is necessary for their own safety, and to prevent their being led into a snare by false teachers and false pretenders to religion; and though it be also beyond doubt that the Scriptures do abound with rules which may be very serviceable to ministers, in counselling and conducting souls committed to their care in things appertaining to their spiritual and eternal state; yet it is also evident, that it was never God's design to give us any rules by which we may *certainly* know who of our fellow professors are His, and to

make a *full and clear* separation between sheep and goats.[19]

This caveat was needful; for in a few short years Edwards would be accused of doing this very thing.

8

Controversy and Dismissal

B y 1743 the Great Awakening in New England had come to a halt. And a year later trouble was stirring in Northampton. In fact, several events coincided to make 1744 a significant year in Edwards' story.

The first sign of trouble was the "bad book case," as it has come to be called. In March of 1744 Edwards was informed that a handbook on midwifery was being circulated among some of the young people. Some boys (or young men) were viewing the diagrams, joking obscenely, and then teasing some of the town's girls. When Edwards learned of the situation, he called for a church meeting and asked for a committee to assist him in investigating the matter. The church agreed. But after the committee was established and a hearing time was set, Edwards read a list of names of those he wanted present. Some of the leading members' children were named. Their parents were shocked—and offended. Edwards had made a blunder in that he did not clarify that some of the youth mentioned were being summoned only as witnesses, not as suspects. According to Serono Dwight, an early Edwards biographer, "the town was suddenly all in a blaze." After two months of intense commotion, two young men, Simeon and Timothy Root, confessed before the church. But the damage had been done. Writing many years later, Dwight commented that after this incident Edwards "greatly lost his influence" in Northampton. There was "no great visible success" in his ministry after this.[1]

The alienation caused by the bad book case was evident in Edwards' battle with the church over his salary. Due to the depreciation of Massachusetts' currency, he had been underpaid for several years. But when in 1744 he asked for a raise, he was stonewalled. It was not until 1748 that his pay was increased, and in the course of the dispute the relationship between pastor and people deteriorated.

The third problem that developed was theological in nature. As seen earlier, Stoddard had taught that an unregenerate person could partake of the Lord's Supper provided he made a profession of faith and avoided flagrant sin. Testimony of a salvation experience was not necessary. As a result, the visible church became a mixed multitude. By 1744 Edwards had come to hold a position on Communion that differed from Stoddard's and from the long-standing practice of Northampton. As we shall see, this difference of opinion would be used later as a pretext for dismissing Edwards as pastor.

In the midst of these conflicts and his many duties as pastor, preacher, and revivalist, Edwards was heartened by close family relationships. His early love and admiration for his wife, Sarah, never abated. She was his perfect "helpmeet." She governed the home in his many absences, orchestrated the chores while he studied, and graciously entertained guests who came to confer or study with her husband. One such guest was Samuel Hopkins, who visited the Northampton parsonage in the winter of 1741, when the Great Awakening was at its height, and who resided there for seven months. As an eyewitness to their relationship, Hopkins noted that "great harmony and mutual love and esteem" sustained husband and wife.[2]

Hopkins also saw how the children were trained and disciplined. In addition to the six children already mentioned, Edwards was to have five more: Susannah (1740), Eunice (1743), Jonathan (1745), Elizabeth (1747) and Pierrepont (1750). With eleven children in the home, order was a virtue; the children had to strictly observe a nine o'clock curfew. "The hour of retirement was firmly kept," wrote Hopkins. Even the older daughters were required to comply; visiting suitors were dismissed by the chime. Nothing was permitted to "intrude on the religion and order of the family."[3] Both parents rarely resorted to corporal punishment. Edwards disciplined his children "with the greatest calmness and commonly without striking a blow." Sarah was equally successful in the exercise of her authority. She taught the children to "obey her cheerfully, without loud, angry words, much less heavy blows."[4]

As with any family, of course, the Edwards' children were not "little angels." They had fallen natures like everyone else. The eldest daughter, Sarah, for instance, had quite a quick temper. And according to an old tradition, when Elihu Parsons came to Edwards asking for her hand in marriage, he reminded Parsons of Sarah's "unpleasant temper." Parsons then asked, "She has grace, I trust?" Edwards replied with wit and wisdom: "I hope she has, but grace can live where you cannot."[5]

During the troubling 1740s Edwards received additional encouragement from his Scottish correspondents. Beginning in 1744 John M'Laurin of Glasgow, James Robe of Kilsyth, Thomas Gillespie, John Erskine, and others, banded together to form a prayer union for the advancement of the gospel. Named the Concert for United Prayer, its design was to form a prayer network for intercession on behalf of the international extension of Christ's kingdom. These men were in dead earnest—seeking worldwide revival through prayer. Their ardent desire was for God to "appear in his glory, and favour Zion, and manifest his compassion to the world of mankind, by an abundant effusion of his Holy Spirit on all the churches and the whole habitable earth, to revive true religion in all parts of Christendom and to deliver all nations from their great and manifold spiritual calamities and miseries. . . ."[6]

As word of the Concert spread throughout Great Britain, John Wesley suggested that Edwards be invited to join. He heartily endorsed the plan. Writing to his friends in Scotland, he said, "Such an agreement and practice appears to me exceeding beautiful, and becoming Christians; and I doubt not but it is so in Christ's eyes."[7] Consequently, Edwards began to take "a great deal of pains to promote this concert here in America"[8] by preaching a series of sermons on Zechariah 8:20–22 and by forming private prayer groups in his church devoted to this purpose. He also revised his sermons for publication; and by January 1748 his book promoting the prayer concert was finally published as *An Humble Attempt to Promote Explicit Agreement and Visible Union of God's People in Extraordinary Prayer, for the Revival of Religion and the Advancement of Christ's Kingdom on Earth, pursuant to Scripture-Promises and Prophecies concerning the*

Last Time. In this work, Edwards uttered his prophetic vision that the gospel of Christ would eventually spread "throughout all parts of Africa, Asia, America and Terra Australis"—a vision that has been largely realized.[9] Though Edwards was undoubtedly discouraged by the passing of the Great Awakening, he never lost faith in the power of the gospel and the promises of God.

Providentially, in May of 1747, just as Edwards was polishing his missionary manuscript for the press, the now famous missionary David Brainerd rode into Northampton. The two had not seen each other since their first and only meeting at the Yale commencement of 1743, although Edwards had kept abreast of Brainerd's brief but blazing career. Around the time of the commencement, the Society in Scotland for Propagating Christian Knowledge hired Brainerd to be a missionary to the American Indians. He was first sent to Kaunaumeek, twenty miles from Stockbridge, on the western borders of Massachusetts and New York. John Sargeant, a former student of Edwards, was working with the Indians at Stockbridge, and during the winter of 1743–1744 he tutored Brainerd in Indian languages. After little visible success, Brainerd was sent to the Indians on the Delaware River in Pennsylvania, and by October he traveled west to the Susquehanna River. The following spring Brainerd was fatigued, ill, and discouraged. While contemplating resignation in the summer of 1745, a revival took place among the Indians at Crossweeksung in New Jersey. For the next several months Brainerd labored furiously, riding three thousand miles on horseback in only nine months. However, he was so ill by late 1746 that he spent the winter months resting at the home of Jonathan Dickinson, then president of Princeton.

When Brainerd arrived in Northampton, in the spring of 1747, his illness (probably tuberculosis) was far advanced. After a brief trip to Boston with Edwards' daughter Jerusha, Brainerd returned to Northampton for his final days. For the next few months he steadily and rapidly deteriorated, and on the morning of October 9, 1747, he died in Edwards' home. Before passing away, however, Brainerd had given his personal diaries and papers to Edwards to dispose of as he "thought would be most for God's glory and the interest of religion."[10] The result was Edwards' *An Account of the Life of the Late Reverend Mr. David Brainerd*. Published in 1749, this work became his most widely read and influential book.

Edwards' sadness at the death of Brainerd was compounded by the loss of two others close to him. The first was his daughter Jerusha. It seems that she served as Brainerd's nurse during his last days in the Northampton parsonage; sadly, she contracted tuberculosis from him. In February 1748 she fell ill. While on her deathbed, she told her family that "she had not seen one minute, for several years, wherein she desired to live one minute longer, for the sake of any other good in life, but doing good, living to God, and doing what might be for his glory." Five days later she died. Thus only four months after Brainerd's death, Jerusha was laid to rest next to him.[11]

The second loss was his uncle John Stoddard (the son of Rev. Solomon Stoddard), who died in June of the same year. Colonel Stoddard had been the chief justice of the county and the leading citizen in Northampton. He reigned over the town like "the squire of an English village. No one else in the community had as much money as he or as much influence. He owned the first teapot in Northampton and the first gold watch."[12] In addition to being a county judge, he was a military commander against the French and the Indians. Despite the conflicts in Northampton in the 1740s, Stoddard's support of Edwards' ministry shielded him from any direct opposition. In the words of Hopkins, Justice Stoddard "greatly strengthened" Edwards' hands. With his departure, however, Edwards lost his most influential backer in the town. Support for his ministry quickly faded. Moreover, now that Stoddard was gone, Edwards' critical cousin Israel Williams became the most prominent figure in the Connecticut Valley. As one biographer put it, Edwards was now "marked for punishment."[13]

The troubles brewing in Northampton now came to a boil in the "Communion controversy." As mentioned earlier, Edwards had come to a position on church membership that differed from Rev. Stoddard's practice at Northampton. In essence, Edwards wanted applicants to make a public profession of saving faith or "godliness," not simply a profession of intellectual assent. Edwards drew up a "form of public profession" that he was willing to accept:

> I hope I truly find in my heart a willingness to comply with all the commandments of God, which require me to give up myself wholly to him, and to serve him with my body and my spirit. And do accordingly now promise to walk in a way of obedience to all the commandments of God, as long as I live.[14]

In December of 1748 an applicant for membership was told by Edwards that he must make a public "profession of godliness." He refused. As word of the incident spread, tension began mounting in the town. Edwards was accused of "lording it over the flock" and of presuming to judge between "sheep and goats." At a church committee meeting in February 1749, Edwards suggested that he preach on the qualifications for membership. The committee objected but then agreed that Edwards should put his views in print. In the meantime, another applicant, Mary Hulbert, came to Edwards for admission. During the interview she expressed her willingness to "publicly make a profession of religion." But by the time she returned for a second interview she told Edwards that based on what she heard from others she was afraid "there would be a tumult if she came into the church in that way. . . ." The issue was then referred to the committee of the church that declined, in April 1749, to approve Hulbert making a public profession.

The dispute was escalating. It was now clear to all that Edwards and his people were at odds on an important doctrinal point. Therefore, Edwards informed the church committee that he would resign his post under two conditions. First, that the current members would wait to read his forthcoming book on the subject before voting; and second, that a "regular council" of ministers would approve his resignation (assuming the dispute could not be resolved). The committee agreed.

Edwards' book arrived in Northampton in August bearing the descriptive title *An Humble Inquiry into the Rules of the Word of God concerning the Qualifications requisite to a Complete Standing and Full Communion in the Visible Christian Church*. In the preface he wrote, "I am conscious, not only is the interest of religion concerned in this affair, but my own reputation, future usefulness, and my very subsistence; all seem to depend on my freely opening and defending myself as to my principles. . . ."[15] Never was Edwards more correct.

For a short time the controversy cooled, but in October 1749 two or three persons were converted and asked for admission to the church. Strife again erupted. A resolution was passed in the town meeting threatening Edwards with dismissal if he persisted in his principles. By December a council of local ministers was convened to hear the dispute. Edwards appealed to the ministers to require his people to hear him preach on the subject since most of them had neglected to read his book. The request was rejected. Seeing the bias of the council due to the influence of the Williams clan, Edwards then asked that, should the conflict between he and his church not be resolved, the next council be composed of some ministers from outside Hampshire County. Again the council refused.

Edwards keenly felt the intense malice toward him. Writing to his friend Joseph Bellamy, he said,

> Things are in great confusion: the tumult is vastly greater than when you were here, and is rising higher and higher continually. The people have got their resentments up to a great height. . . .
>
> I need God's counsel in every step I take and every word I speak; as all that I do and say is watched by the multitude around me with the utmost strictness and with eyes of the greatest uncharitableness and severity, and let me do or say what I will, my words and actions are represented in dark colours, and the state of things is come to that . . . that they seem to think it greatly concerns them to blacken me and represent me in odious colours to the world to justify their own conduct; they seem to be sensible that now their character can't stand unless it be on the ruin of mine.[16]

The hostility toward Edwards could hardly be the result of the doctrinal question in dispute. Rather, old resentment now had a pretense for spewing out its venom. Many of Edwards' opponents were related to the Williams family, and with Colonel Stoddard's death, Israel Williams became the chief citizen of Hampshire County. It was Williams, it should be remembered, who had bitterly attacked Edwards back in 1734 for preaching against Arminianism. Four other ministers in the county were also part of the Williams family. Moreover, Joseph Hawley Jr., who took an active role against Edwards, had lost his father to suicide during the revival of 1734–1735. His attitude toward Edwards may have been colored by this event, as well as by the fact that Hawley had, in 1747, been at odds with Edwards on a case of church discipline involving his brother, Elisha. Deacon Pomeroy, another opponent of Edwards, had likewise sided with Hawley in the discipline case. Thus there was by 1748 a close-knit faction that disliked Edwards for personal reasons. Moreover, the great offense caused by the "bad book case," and the bad blood generated by the salary dispute, had made Edwards "obnoxious" to his people.

After another council meeting in early February 1750, it was decided that Edwards would preach on the controversy during the Thursday lectures. Angry at Edwards having a hearing, Noah Cook and Ebenezer Pomeroy sent a letter of protest to Chester Williams, a representative of the Hampshire Association of Ministers. The ministers convened briefly but took no action, so Edwards gave his lectures as scheduled. He began on February 15 and delivered five lectures, which were sparsely attended by his own congregation, although many visitors were present. At the March 25 church meeting, a great majority indicated that their views on the subject had not changed; thus, it was now necessary to choose a ministerial council to decide Edwards' fate. Desiring a fair hearing, Edwards demanded that he have a hand in choosing the members of the council. (He was clearly trying to avoid the predominance of the Williams family in Hampshire.) Not until May 3 was the question settled: The future council would include at least two ministers, chosen by Edwards, from outside of Hampshire.

The decisive council convened in Northampton on June 19, 1750, and met for four days. They called a special church meeting, in which the people voted on Edwards' dismissal. Led by Joseph Hawley Jr., a heated majority voted for his removal. Though a minority of the council protested the people's hastiness, it was decided by a vote of ten to nine that Edwards' pastoral relation to Northampton church should be ended. Thus after twenty-three years of diligent ministry Edwards was publicly rejected by the people he had so faithfully served and so dearly loved.

Edwards received the verdict unshaken. As David Hall, a member of the council, jotted in his diary, "I never saw the least symptoms of displeasure in his countenance the whole week, but he appeared like a man of God, whose happiness was out of the reach of his enemies. . . ."[17]

On July 1, 1750, only nine days after his dismissal, Edwards had to face his accusers and deliver a farewell sermon. Basing his message on 2 Corinthians 1:14, "As also ye have acknowledged us in part, that we are your rejoicing, even as ye also are ours in the day of the Lord Jesus," he advised his former flock that both pastor and parishioners would one day stand before the judgment seat of Christ. At that day, God would examine the conduct of each in their respective treatment of one another. For his own part, Edwards reminded the church that he had spent the best years of his life laboring on their behalf:

I have spent the prime of my life and strength in labours for your eternal welfare. You are my witnesses that what strength I have had, I have not neglected in idleness . . . but have given myself to the work of the ministry, labouring in it night and day, rising early, and applying myself to this great business to which Christ has appointed me. . . .

He also admonished them for their contentious spirit. "The contentions which have been among you, since I first became your pastor, have been one of the greatest burdens I have laboured under in the course of my ministry. . . ." This spirit, he warned, would "tend to drive away God's Spirit" from the church. "Let this late contention about the terms of Christian communion, as it has been the greatest, be the last."

Edwards then expressed his desire for their future welfare, asking that God might bless them with a faithful pastor, "one that is well acquainted with His mind and will, thoroughly warning sinners, wisely and skillfully searching professors and conducting you in the way to eternal blessedness. . . ." And finally, "Let us all remember, and never forget our future solemn meeting on the great day of the Lord; the day of infallible decision and of the everlasting and unalterable sentence. Amen."[18]

Many were moved by his tender but solemn address. Some were "much affected, and some are exceedingly grieved," noted Edwards. There may have even been "some relentings of heart" that they "voted me away."[19]

Such remorse notwithstanding, Edwards was to go.

9

Missionary and Theologian

D ismissal from the Northampton church left
Edwards and his family without any visible
means of support and with no future prospects
of employment. Writing in early July to his friend
John Erskine, Edwards mused on his precarious situation: "I am now, as it were, thrown upon the wide
ocean of the world, and know not what will become of
me and my numerous and chargeable family. Nor have
I any particular door in view that I depend upon to be
opened for my future serviceableness. . . ." Despite the
harsh treatment of his former flock, and the unpromising outlook for the immediate future, Edwards
steadfastly trusted in God: "We are in the hands of
God, and I bless him, I am not anxious concerning his
disposal."[1]

For the next several months Edwards was unemployed. At the same time the Northampton church
was without a pastor, the supply committee having
been unable to locate a suitable replacement. So,
strange as it sounds, Edwards was asked to occasionally fill the pulpit when another preacher could not be
recruited. This he did at least twelve times over the
next several months. On one occasion, two strangers

who were prejudiced against Edwards visited Northampton and attended the Sabbath service. Since they
had never actually seen Edwards, they assumed the
preacher that day was someone else. In the course of
the sermon, one of the strangers whispered to his
friend, "This is a *good* man." A little later in the sermon he leaned over and whispered again, "This is a
very good man." Near the end, he was heard to say,
"Whoever he may be, this is a *holy* man."[2]

Unfortunately, the majority at Northampton did
not share the stranger's admiration for Edwards. Opponents objected to his supplying the pulpit, and the
hostility toward him continued unabated. At a town
meeting a vote was passed to deny him the use of the
public grazing land, and it was finally agreed in November that it would be better to have no preacher at
all than to have Edwards. He was plainly being rail-
roaded out of town. "So deep were their prejudices
that their heat was maintained; nothing would quiet
them till they could see the town clear of root and
branch, name and remnant."[3]

A month later Edwards received a call to the Stockbridge Indian Settlement, which had been founded as
a missionary project of the Society in London for Propagating the Gospel in New England. Colonel Stoddard, John Sargeant, and Edwards himself had been
present at a meeting in Stoddard's home in 1734 when
the decision was made to launch the settlement. It is
not surprising, then, that Edwards entertained the invitation to labor there.

Accordingly, on a snowy day in January 1751, Edwards trekked to Stockbridge to inspect the situation
firsthand. During the two-month visit he found a
small but thriving frontier village. About two hundred
Housatonic Indians lived there, with a school for their

children run by Timothy Woodbridge. There was also a separate boarding school for the Mohawks, both young and old, run by a Captain John Kellogg. The church in Stockbridge was comprised of only a handful of white families and a slightly larger number of Indians.

The prospect of laboring like Brainerd as a missionary to the Indians was attractive to Edwards. For many years he had a genuine concern for the salvation and welfare of the American Indian. Stockbridge seemed to offer an ideal outlet for Edwards' vision of missionary expansion, except for the fact that there were several obstacles to such a move. First, there was no parsonage in Stockbridge, and Edwards had no money to build one. Second, his potential salary would be far less than before. Third, Edwards knew no Indian language and would have to work through an interpreter. But the most important objection to moving to Stockbridge was the fact that a branch of the Williams family lived there. The leading landowner (400 acres) in Stockbridge was Ephraim Williams, an uncle of Solomon Williams, who differed with Edwards on the Communion question and who had published a reply to Edwards' *Humble Inquiry*. Ephraim's daughter, Abigail, had been married to John Sargeant; and his son, Ephraim Jr., was the town's representative to the General Court.

Back in Northampton, by March, Edwards undoubtedly discussed the Stockbridge proposal with his wife, and they both surely sought the throne of grace for guidance. During the next few months Edwards' friends in Scotland sent him financial help; and, probably much to Edwards' surprise, they asked him and his wife to sit for portraits. Thankfully, Jonathan and Sarah cooperated immediately, and their portraits, now a great treasure to the church, were finished by the autumn of 1751. In the meantime some of Edwards' friends in Northampton proposed a second church in town, with Edwards as pastor. Though he objected to the idea, his critics accused him of scheming to reestablish himself in Northampton and of dividing the existing church. This last attack was the worst. "Such is the state of things among us," wrote Edwards, "that a person cannot appear on my side without exposing himself to the resentments of his friends and neighbours, and being the object of much odium."[4]

Now convinced that it would be best for his family if they left town, Edwards went to Stockbridge in July, and was officially installed as pastor on August 8, 1751. Sarah and the children soon followed in October. His family, by this time, was blessed with a third boy, Pierrepont. Also, his daughter Sarah had married Elihu Parsons in June 1750, and two months later Mary wed Timothy Dwight. Elihu and Sarah likewise moved to Stockbridge, while the Dwights stayed in Northampton. In protest of her father's dismissal, Mary never again took Communion at the church.

Just as Edwards was getting settled in his new position, he again became embroiled in conflict. In early 1752 the Boston Commissioners sent Gideon Hawley to Stockbridge to assume the oversight of the Mohawk school. Captain Kellogg, the current director, had mismanaged the school for some time and was misappropriating funds sent from England. Not surprisingly, he contested his dismissal and resisted Hawley. Strife broke out, with Williams supporting Kellogg and Edwards supporting Hawley. By summer Elisha Williams, a recently appointed member of the Boston Commission, arrived in Stockbridge and demanded that Edwards answer directly to him. Edwards refused, insisting he was answerable to the entire commission, not just one of its members. Ill will increased to such a point that by the winter of 1752 Joseph Dwight (Abigail Williams' new husband) was petitioning the General Court in an attempt to have Edwards removed. Simultaneously, Ephraim Williams Sr. was trying to buy the land titles of Edwards' white friends in order to move them out of town. In February 1753 the Mohawk school, now under the oversight of Gideon Hawley, mysteriously burned to the ground. All of Hawley's personal possessions were destroyed. Two months later he left town, with many Mohawks following. After nearly another year of discord, the Boston Commission finally sided with Edwards. "He won a complete victory," writes Arthur McGiffert. "His persuasiveness and aggressiveness, reinforced by his reputation for integrity, saved the mission from further exploitation. . . . Ultimately he was himself given charge of the mission station, its funds, and its staff."[5]

Edwards also endured other difficulties on the frontier. The first problem was financial. The cost of moving to Stockbridge, the expense of marrying two daughters, and his smaller missionary salary left Edwards in debt. In fact, Edwards was so desperate for a study notebook that he sewed together any miscellaneous scraps of paper he could find. "Printer's proofs, old proclamations of intended marriages from Northampton days, envelopes, letters, and much else, could all be utilized, even if there was only room on the margins or the bottoms of sheets."[6] His daughters, in order to help out, took up lace-making, embroidery, and fan-painting, and sold their wares in Boston.

Another trial was family sickness. In late 1752 Edwards' wife, Sarah, was so ill that she nearly died. His daughter Betty "was brought nigh unto death," and Sarah Parsons likewise was very sick.[7] Edwards himself fell ill in the summer of 1754 with a case of malaria that lasted until January of the next year.

Of course the perennial problem on the frontier was the threat of Indian attacks. At the same time that Edwards was sick, some Indians from Canada swept into Stockbridge on a Sabbath and killed four men. The French-Indian War was just heating up, making Stockbridge a vulnerable frontier target. During these years it was not uncommon for soldiers to be garrisoned at Edwards' home. He read his Bible to the rattle of bayonets.

In spite of all these obstacles, Edwards faithfully toiled as a missionary and theologian. He commonly conducted four services on the Sabbath: one for the Housatonics, one for the Mohawks, and two for his small white congregation. When preaching to the Indians, Edwards had to aim at simplicity, as can be seen from the sermon notes of one of his Indian sermons. Preaching on 2 Timothy 3:16, Edwards said,

'Tis worth the while to take a great deal of pains to learn to read and understand the Scriptures.

I would have all of you think of this.

When there is such a book that you may have, how can you be contented without being able to read it?

How does it make you feel when you think there is a Book that is God's own Word? . . .

You must not only hear it read, etc., but you must have it sink down into your heart. Believe. Be affected. Love the Word of God.

You must not only read and hear, but DO the things. Otherwise it will do no good; you will be the worse for it.

Consider how much it is worth the while to go often to your Bible to hear the great God Himself speak to you.[8]

During the week, Edwards taught classes on the Westminster catechism and sacred history and instructed both white and Indian children in writing and spelling. There is certainly something touching, and ironic, in seeing America's most astute theologian tutoring children in their alphabet. Edwards, however, valuing humility as he did, was not above becoming a little child for Christ's sake.

In some ways the move to Stockbridge, despite the hardships, was an unsought blessing. Compared to the bustle of activity and the burden of ministry in Northampton, Edwards' remote post was relatively quiet. There were fewer visitors to entertain and a smaller congregation to shepherd. God, in His good providence, provided Edwards with more time for deep theological reflection and study (and the result would prove a rich blessing to the future church).

At Stockbridge, Edwards devoted himself to writing his greatest theological books. In November 1752 he published his last statement on the Communion controversy, entitled *Misrepresentations Corrected*. Shortly thereafter, in August of the same year, he began writing his *Careful and Strict Inquiry into the Modern Prevailing Notions of the Freedom of Will which is supposed to be Essential to Moral Agency*. Directed at the work of Thomas Chubb, Daniel Whitby, and Isaac Watts, it was Edwards' aim to refute the Arminian notion of human liberty and to show how God's sovereignty could be compatible with human responsibility. This massive and intricate work has four sections. The first deals with the definition of such terms as "necessity," "contingency," "liberty," and many others. Part 2 is a critique of the Arminian view of liberty. Part 3 contains a discussion of whether freedom is essential to praise or blame. And in part 4, Edwards handles the arguments of his opponents.

Throughout the work, Edwards attempts to establish or prove two theses. First, he argues that God's certain foreknowledge of all that happens is inconsistent with the existence of contingency. Second, he argues that the volitions of the human soul of Jesus were necessarily holy, yet could still be called virtuous and praiseworthy. Scholar John E. Smith noted:

> The first of these theses was directed against the belief in self-determination or freedom of the will, which Edwards associated with the Arminian thinkers. The second was meant to refute the belief that what is necessitated cannot be the object of praise or blame. The entire argument of the *Freedom of the Will* is directed to the establishment of these two claims. . . .[9]

Whether or not one agrees with Edwards' conclusions, Perry Miller is correct in suggesting that this work alone, due to its metaphysical majesty, was enough to establish Edwards as America's greatest philosopher-theologian.[10]

In the winter and spring of 1754–1755, Edwards composed two dissertations: *A Dissertation concerning the End for which God created the World* and *A Dissertation concerning the Nature of True Virtue.* Intended to be read together, the two are Edwards' answer to the Enlightenment's attempt to define virtue or morality apart from God. While some writers, such as Francis Hutcheson, acknowledged God in their ethical systems, it is clear that Hutcheson did not think God was foundational to morality. Edwards wrote,

> There seems to be an inconsistency in some writers on morality, in this respect, that they do not wholly exclude a regard to the Deity out of their schemes of morality, but yet mention it so slightly, that they leave me room and reason to suspect they

esteem it a less important and subordinate part of morality.[11]

In effect, the trend of European moral philosophy at the time was to first limit, and then exclude, God from questions of morality.

Edwards, on the other hand, answered by saying that this approach was an inversion of the true order; namely, that we are required to love God first and supremely, and mankind secondarily:

> And it may be asserted in general, that nothing is of the nature of true virtue, in which God is not the *first* and *last*; or which, with regard to their exercises in general, have not their first foundation and source in apprehensions of God's supreme dignity and glory, and in answerable esteem and love of him, and have not respect to God as the supreme end.[12]

Edwards' last major theological work, *The Great Christian Doctrine of Original Sin Defended*, was started in 1756 and published in early 1758. The occasion of the book was twofold. First, Edwards was responding to John Taylor's book *The Scripture-Doctrine of Original Sin Proposed to Free and Candid Examination*. But perhaps more significantly, Edwards saw the Enlightenment bias, which ignored man's innate depravity and exalted his inherent goodness. But if man is not a sinner, then he needs no atonement, no gospel, and no Christ. Using both reason and revelation, Edwards established an arsenal of arguments showing that all men—civilized Europeans and savage Indians alike—are indeed sinners in need of Christ's atonement.

While working on *Original Sin*, Edwards received a letter from Aaron Burr, president of the College of New Jersey (now Princeton), informing him of a revival at the school. Burr, it should be mentioned, was also Edwards' son-in-law, having married his daughter Esther in September of 1752. Over the years Burr and Edwards had stayed in contact, and on several occasions Edwards had visited the college. In September 1755, for instance, Edwards was the guest speaker at the college commencement. When word arrived in February 1757 of the awakening among the students, Edwards was overjoyed and passed on the good news to his friends in Scotland.

Unfortunately, Edwards' joy was short-lived. Six months later he learned that Governor Belcher, a strong supporter of the school, had passed away. Then, to the shock of everyone connected with the institution, Burr himself died a month later at the age of forty-one. Esther, his bereaved widow, found her solace in God. Writing home to Stockbridge, she commented on God's grace to her during this tragic time: "God has seemed sensibly near in such a supporting and comfortable manner that I think I have never experienced the like."[13]

Only four days after Burr's death, Princeton's Board of Trustees chose Edwards as his successor. When news arrived in Stockbridge, Edwards wrote a long letter (dated October 19, 1757) stating his objections to the invitation. First, Edwards thought the move to Princeton would be a discomfort to his family, especially since they had only recently settled in Stockbridge. Another move, he thought, might produce further financial strain as well. More important, Edwards felt that he was unfit for the position of president:

> The chief difficulties in my mind, in the way of accepting this important and arduous office, are these two: First, my own defects unfitting me for such an undertaking, many of which are generally known; be-

sides others of which my own heart is conscious—I have a constitution, in many respects, peculiarly unhappy, attended with . . . a low tide of spirits; often occasioning a kind of childish weakness and contemptibleness of speech, presence, and demeanour, with a disagreeable dullness and stiffness, much unfitting me for conversation, but more especially for the government of a college. This makes me shrink at the thought of taking upon me, in the decline of life, such a new and great business, attended with such a multiplicity of cares, and requiring such a degree of activity, alertness, and spirit of government; especially as succeeding one so remarkably well qualified in these respects, giving occasion to everyone to remark on the wide difference. I am also deficient in some parts of learning, particularly in algebra, and the higher parts of mathematics, and the Greek classics; my Greek learning having been chiefly in the New Testament.[14]

Edwards then informed the trustees that he was thoroughly enjoying his reclusive studies and had no desire to be taken from his books: "My engaging in this business will not well consist with those views, and that course of employ in my study, which has long engaged and swallowed up my mind, and been the chief entertainment and delight of my life." In addition to continued projects relating to the debate between Arminians and Calvinists, Edwards was also planning a new work on the subject of divinity:

I have had on my mind and heart (which I long ago began, not with any view to publication) a great work, which I call a *History of the Work of Redemption*, a body of divinity in an entirely new method, being thrown into the form of a history; considering the affair of Christian theology, as the whole of it, each part, stands in reference to the great work of redemption by Jesus Christ; which I suppose to be, of all others, the grand design of God, and the *summum* and *ultimum* of all the divine operations and decrees; particularly considering all parts of the grand scheme, in their historical order.[15]

Edwards concludes his objections by mentioning another work, *A Harmony of the Old and New Testaments*, and writing,

> So far as I myself am able to judge of what talents I have for benefiting my fellow creatures by word, I think I can write better than I can speak. My heart is so much in these studies that I cannot find it in my heart to be willing to put myself into an incapacity to pursue them any more in the future part of my life.[16]

Nevertheless, Edwards did mention that if he should ever come to accept the position, he would only do the work of a professor of divinity. And, if the trustees still wanted to pursue the matter with him, he would seek the advice of some trusted friends.

In light of Edwards' outstanding gifts as a theologian and philosopher, it is not surprising that Princeton persisted in its invitation. Accordingly, Edwards kept his word and called a council of friends to advise him on the matter. Samuel Hopkins, John Brainerd, and Joseph Bellamy were asked to come to Stockbridge in late December 1757. Due to weather, perhaps, the council was briefly delayed and finally met on January 4, 1758. After Edwards presented his view of the matter, Timothy Woodbridge also gave his arguments for keeping Edwards at Stockbridge. In spite of their persuasive pleading, the council informed Edwards that it was his duty to accept the call to Princeton.

He was stunned and broke into tears. Nevertheless, believing that he was bound to heed their advice, he submitted to their counsel and prepared to depart for Princeton. In late January Edwards gave his last

Stockbridge sermon, on the words "We have no continuing city, therefore let us seek one to come." Little did he realize when he made that wintry trip to Princeton just how prophetic those words would prove to be.

10

Farewell and Vindication

Edwards was officially installed as president of Princeton College on February 16, 1758. Despite his previous apprehensions, Edwards settled into his new routine with alacrity. His duties included preaching on the Sabbath in the College hall and quizzing the senior class on questions of theology. As an example, he might ask his students the following questions:

- How do you prove the natural perfection of God, viz. His intelligence, infinite power, foreknowledge, and immutability?
- How do you prove the divinity of Christ?
- What is the true idea of God's decrees?
- Are the law and the gospel inconsistent with each other?
- What is the covenant of redemption?
- What is regeneration?
- What is pardon and justification? What is their foundation, and what is the influence of faith therein?[1]

By all accounts, the students were thrilled with his instruction.

A week after his installation Edwards was advised

to be inoculated for smallpox. Since the disease was then prevalent, and Edwards had not before contracted it, he complied. For a brief time all seemed well, but several weeks later he came down with the disease and his health rapidly declined. He was unable to take fluids, and a fever ravished his body. As he wrestled with death, Edwards called for his daughter Lucy, to whom he said,

> Dear Lucy, it seems to me to be the will of God, that I must shortly leave you; therefore, give my kindest love to my dear wife, and tell her that the uncommon union, which has so long subsisted between us, has been of such a nature, as I trust is spiritual, and therefore will continue forever. And I hope she will be supported under so great a trial and submit cheerfully to the will of God. And as to my children, you are now like to be left fatherless, which I hope will be an inducement to you all to seek a Father who will never fail you.[2]

Now sensing that his departure was near, Edwards looked about the room at his gathered friends and family members, and said, "Now, where is Jesus of Nazareth, my true and never-failing friend?" He then fell into a semi-conscious state. Observing this, and thinking he had died, those at his bedside began to grieve. Then, unexpectedly, Edwards exclaimed, "Trust in God, and you need not fear!" Thus on March 22, 1758, Edwards gave his final witness to the glorious God he had faithfully served for many years.

Edwards' doctor, William Shippen, then wrote to Sarah of her husband's passing.

> *Princeton,*
> *March 22, 1758*
> *Most Dear and Very Worthy Madam,*
> *I am heartily sorry for the occasion of writing to you by this express, but I know you have been informed*

by a line from your excellent, lovely, and pious husband, that I was brought here to inoculate him, and your dear daughter Esther, and her children, for the smallpox, which was then spreading fast in Princeton; and that after the most deliberate and serious consultation, with his nearest and most religious friends, he was accordingly inoculated with them the 23d of last month; and although he had the smallpox favorably, yet, having a number of them in the roof of his mouth and throat, he could not possibly swallow a sufficient quantity of drink, to keep off a secondary fever, which has proved too strong for his feeble frame; and this afternoon, between two and three o'clock, it pleased God to let him sleep in that dear Lord Jesus, whose kingdom and interest he has been faithfully and painfully serving all his life. And never did any mortal man more fully and clearly evidence the sincerity of all his professions, by one continued, universal, calm, cheerful resignation, and patient submission to the Divine will, through every stage of his disease, than he; not so much as one discontented expression, nor the least appearance of murmuring, through the whole. And never did any person expire with more perfect freedom from pain;—not so much as one distorted hair—but in the most proper sense of the words, he fell asleep. Death had certainly lost its sting, as to him.

I conclude, with my hearty prayer, dear Madam, that you may be enabled to look to that God, whose love and goodness you have experienced a thousand times, for direction and help, under this most afflictive dispensation of his providence, and under every other difficulty you may meet with here, in order to your being more perfectly fitted for the joys of heaven hereafter.[3]

Sarah Edwards' response, written to Esther in Princeton, shows both the depth of her faith in God and her insight that, though her husband was now dead, his work would continue.

Stockbridge,
April 3, 1758
My Very Dear Child,
   What shall I say? A holy and good God has covered
us with a dark cloud. O that we may kiss the rod, and
lay our hands on our mouths! The Lord has done it.
He has made me adore his goodness, that we had him
so long. But my God lives; and he has my heart. O
what a legacy my husband, and your father, has left
us! We are all given to God; and there I am, and love
to be.[4]

A day after his death Edwards was given a simple burial at Princeton. Six months later Sarah joined her beloved husband in his grave.

By Colonial standards Edwards lived a full and rich life. He had been an instructor, a pastor, a revivalist, a missionary, a theologian-philosopher, and a college president. He was a powerful instrument in the most powerful revival of his day, and a leading polemicist in the leading controversies of his time. He was a spiritual giant in a day when spirituality was highly prized: a burning and shining star amid a constellation of lesser lights. He had an "uncommon union" with his beloved wife and delighted in the familial fellowship of his many children. His quiver was full; his life had been blessed.

When Edwards died he had no regrets, only expectation. His unfinished manuscripts were mere shadows compared to the light that lay before him. Loving Jesus as he did—his "true and never-failing friend"—Edwards welcomed death as the gateway to everlasting joy. Being his whole life so heavenly minded, how could he now mind going to heaven?

Edwards' unexpected death at the hand of his own

physician, as well as his short-lived tenure as president of Princeton, may seem a tragic ending to such a noble life. Yet we are in God's hands, and how he disposes of His servants is beyond our finite grasp. Why David Brainerd, for instance, should die of tuberculosis at the height of his missionary activity, or Edwards should succumb to a vaccine when on the brink of national, if not international, recognition as a college president and theologian, are questions no one can answer. The secret things belong to the Lord. It is enough for us to answer with Sarah, "The Lord has done it." And there we must rest our faith.

The real tragedy of Edwards' life was not his untimely death by a freak medical accident, or the unfinished work he left behind, or (as some historians suggest) his opposition to the spirit of his age. No, the real tragedy of Edwards' life was that he was underappreciated and even mistreated by those he had loyally served. The Northampton dismissal was, as Edwards knew, a blot on his reputation and a shameful example of the blackest ingratitude. It would have been painful enough to have been separated from the flock he had served for so many years, but Edwards was dismissed under a cloud of false accusations. A "heap of slanders," as he put it, were thrust upon him; and he lived for many years under the dark shadow of suspicion:

> The removal of a minister from his people ordinarily lays him under great disadvantages and commonly hurts his reputation though indeed he be not to blame. There is left on the minds of the world some suspicion, whether something or other blameworthy or unhappy in him, his temper or conduct, was not the cause.[5]

God does, however, honor those who honor Him.

He vindicates the memory of the righteous. And in Edwards' case his vindication began before he died. His banishment to Stockbridge proved a boon to both himself and the church. While secluded from refined society, he composed some of the most refined theological and philosophical works ever written. What men had meant for evil, God meant for good. In addition, his appointment as president of Princeton, though brief, was an unsought honor that demonstrated that God had not forgotten him in the frontier wilderness. Although Edwards would have been content to finish his days as a humble missionary, God chose to remove him from a place of exile to establish him in a chair of esteem. God then received him into a mansion of excellence.

After Edwards' death, the Communion controversy continued in New England, and eventually his position on the subject was vindicated. As it turned out, those churches that adopted his position retained their orthodoxy, while those who rejected it became progressively more liberal. As one historian has noted: "Every Congregational church in New England, probably, has either adopted that doctrine, or become Unitarian. The future destiny of each of the churches seems to have depended more on its treatment of this question, than on any other single event."[6] It was Edwards' position on church membership and Communion that eventually altered the practice of Congregational churches throughout America.

Moreover, in May 1760, a letter of repentance by Joseph Hawley Jr., Edwards' chief antagonist, was printed in a Boston newspaper at his request. It fully vindicates Edwards:

In the course of that most melancholy contention with Mr. Edwards, I now see that I was very much influenced by vast pride, self-sufficiency, ambition, and vanity. I appear to myself vile, and doubtless much more so to others who are more impartial. . . . Such treatment of Mr. Edwards, wherein I was so deeply concerned and active, was particularly and very aggravatedly sinful and ungrateful in me, because I was not only under the common obligations of each individual of the society to him, as a most able, diligent and faithful pastor; but I had also received many instances of his tenderness, goodness and generosity to me as a young kinsman, whom he was disposed to treat in a most friendly manner. . . . I am most sorely sensible that nothing but that infinite grace and mercy which saved some of the betrayers and murderers of our blessed Lord, and the persecutors of his martyrs, can pardon me; in which alone I hope for pardon, for the sake of Christ, whose blood, blessed be God, cleanseth from all sin.[7]

Years later Hawley imitated his father's demise. He committed suicide.

The other great controversy that engaged much of Edwards' energy was the Great Awakening. Indeed, to this very day, historians are divided, as were the original disputants, over the value of the Awakening. This would not have surprised Edwards. Stumbling blocks were inevitable: James Davenport's descendants lived on. Nevertheless, much good came out of the revival. It is estimated that as many as twenty to fifty thousand souls came to Christ through the preaching of Edwards, Whitefield, Tennent, and many others. This alone should justify their labors. In addition, the evangelistic zeal of the original revivalists spread far and wide throughout the Colonies and the Old World. The modern missionary movement was partially inspired by Edwards' own example as a revivalist and missionary, his *Life of Brainerd*, and his revival writings. The aftershocks of the Great Awakening were felt also in higher education. Yale gave birth to the modern student movement, and Princeton was the home of such Edwardsean heirs as Charles Hodge and B. B. Warfield.

Perhaps the ultimate vindication of Edwards' life and work is the continued influence he exerts through the written word. Shortly after his death, Samuel Hopkins wrote a brief biography of Edwards, which he prefaced to the publication of some of Edwards' sermons. He then published the *Two Dissertations* in 1765. In England, John Wesley was abridging and publishing *A Faithful Narrative, Some Thoughts on the Revival, Religious Affections*, and the *Life of Brainerd*. Five new titles of Edwards were published in Scotland, and when William Carey was sent out to India in 1793, he carried a volume of Edwards with him.

By 1810 a set of Edwards' works was published and had a profound influence on some of the most successful and well-known preachers of the day—men such as Edward Payson, Edward D. Griffin, Lyman Beecher, and others. The latter once counseled his son, "Next after the Bible, read and study Edwards, whom to understand in theology, accommodated to use, will be as high praise in theological science as to understand Newton's works in accommodation to modern uses of natural philosophy." The Scots divine Thomas Chalmers eulogized Edwards' writings thus:

> There is no European Divine to whom I make such frequent appeals in my classrooms as I do to Edwards.
>
> I have long esteemed him as the greatest of theologians, combining, in a degree that is quite unexampled, the profoundly intellectual with the devot-

edly spiritual and sacred, and realizing in his own person a most rare yet most beautiful harmony between the simplicity of the Christian pastor on the one hand, and, on the other, all the strength and prowess of a giant in philosophy; so as at once to minister from Sabbath to Sabbath, and with the most blessed effect, to the hearers of his plain congregation, and yet in the high field of authorship to have traversed, in a way that none had ever done before him, the most inaccessible places, and achieved such a mastery as had never till his time been realized over the most arduous difficulties of our science.[8]

To this very day Edwards' works are being reprinted, read, studied, and discussed by both theologians and philosophers. Even his alma mater, Yale, which has fallen prey to liberalism and secularism, is editing a definitive edition of his collective works.

Finally, Edwards continues to influence average Christian men and women by the power of his godly example. While his books are masterpieces of exposition, his life was a masterwork of devotion. From the day of his conversion to the end of his life, he lived in the light of God and of eternity. He solemnly dedicated himself to God's glory and conducted his entire life with a view to fulfilling his vow. The key to Edwards is knowing the power of consecration. He gave everything to God: his mind, his body, and his soul. He offered himself as a living sacrifice. He resolved to strive in all ways and at all times to please God. He counted all things as refuse compared to the excellency of Christ, whom he loved above all others. Not content to flicker as a candle, he burned as the sun, giving light to all around him.

Fortunately for us, the light continues to shine to this day.

Chronology of Edwards' Life and Writings

1703, October 5—Jonathan Edwards born at East Windsor, Connecticut

1708–1709—Edwards has first "religious experience" during revival in his father's church.

1713—Edwards writes paper attacking materialism.

1716—Earliest letter to sister (May 10); essay "Of Insects" supposedly written at this time

1716, September—Enrolls in Yale

1720—Graduates Yale

1720–1722—Remains at Yale as graduate student

1721—Writes "Of Being"

1721, Spring—Conversion experience

1722, August—Edwards becomes minister of small Presbyterian church in New York; stays only eight months. Develops "Resolutions"

1723—Writes "The Mind" and "Apostrophe to Sarah Pierrepont"

1723, April—Leaves New York parish and spends summer with his parents

1723, September—Returns to Yale, receives M.A. degree

1724, May—Appointed tutor at Yale. Takes up residence in June

1725—Writes "Beauty of the World"

1725, September—Edwards suffers severe illness, lasting three months; never recovers former strength

1726, August—Receives call to Northampton

1726, September—Resigns as tutor at Yale

1727, February 22—Ordained as associate pastor of Northampton congregation under the pastorate of Solomon Stoddard, his maternal grandfather

1727, July 28—Edwards, twenty-three years old, marries Sarah Pierrepont, then seventeen. Sarah's father was a founder of Yale and framer of the Saybrook Platform.

1728—Writes "Images of Divine Things"

1729, February—Death of Solomon Stoddard. Edwards becomes pastor of Northampton church.

1729, Spring—Breakdown of Edwards' health

1731, July 8—Edwards gives public lecture in Boston, published as *God Glorified in Man's Dependence*.

1734—Edwards preaches controversial sermons on justification and is criticized by Williams side of family.

1734, December—Revival begins in Northampton. Preaches "A Divine and Supernatural Light" and "Discourses on Various Subjects"

1735, April—Revival reaches its height; Joseph Hawley, Edwards' uncle, commits suicide.

1735, Fall—Edwards takes vacation for health reasons; travels to New York and New Jersey and meets the Tennents.

1737, Fall—Publication in London of *Faithful Narrative*

1738—Preaches "Charity and Its Fruits"; publishes *Discourses on Various Subjects*

1738—George Whitefield arrives in America.

1739—Publication of "A History of the Work of Redemption." Composes "Personal Narrative"

1740, October 17—Whitefield visits Edwards and preaches at Northampton.

1741, July—Revival progresses. Edwards preaches famous sermon "Sinners in the Hands of an Angry God" at Enfield.

1741, September—Edwards at Yale commencement; Samuel Hopkins first hears Edwards there. New Haven sermon "Distinguishing Marks"

1741, December—Edwards on "missionary tour." Hopkins arrives at parsonage, stays six to seven months.

1742, January—Edwards again away preaching (Leicester)

1742, February—Returns to Northampton to find Sarah "revived"

1743, March—Revival begins to subside. Publication of *Some Thoughts Concerning the Present Revival*

1743—Charles Chauncy, pastor of First Church of Boston, publishes *Seasonable Thoughts* against revival.

1744—Troubles begin at Northampton: bad book case, dispute over salary.

1744, October—Start of International Union

1746—Publication of *A Treatise Concerning the Religious Affections*

1747, May 28—David Brainerd arrives at Northampton.

1747, October 9—Death of Brainerd

1748, January—Publication of *An Humble Attempt*

1748, February—Death of Edwards' daughter Jerusha

1749—Publication of *An Account of the Life of Brai-*

nerd and *An Humble Inquiry*

1750, June 22—Edwards dismissed from Northampton pastorate.

1750, July—Farewell sermon

1750, December—Edwards receives call to Stockbridge missionary settlement.

1751, August 8—Edwards officially installed at Stockbridge. Conflict with Williams family

1752, November—Publication of *Misrepresentations Corrected*

1754—Publication of *Freedom of the Will*

1754, July–December—Edwards seriously ill with fever

1755—Edwards writes *Nature of True Virtue* and *End for Which God Created the World*; both published posthumously.

1756–1763—Seven Years' War between England and France

1757, September 24—Edwards' son-in-law, Aaron Burr, president of the College of New Jersey (Princeton) dies. Edwards called to be president.

1758—Publication of *Original Sin*

1758, February 16—Edwards installed as president of Princeton.

1758, February 23—Edwards inoculated for smallpox.

1758, March 22—Edwards dies from smallpox. Six months later his wife, Sarah, dies. Both are buried at Princeton.

Select Bibliography

Ahlstrom, Sydney E. *A Religious History of the American People*. New Haven and London: Yale University Press, 1973.

Aldridge, Alfred Owen. *Jonathan Edwards*. New York: Washington Square Press, Inc., 1966.

Bickel, R. Bruce. *Light and Heat*. Morgan, Pa.: Soli Deo Gloria Publications, 1999.

Dallimore, Arnold. *George Whitefield*, 2 vols. Edinburgh: The Banner of Truth Trust, 1970.

Edwards, Jonathan. *The Works of Jonathan Edwards*, 2 vols. Edinburgh: The Banner of Truth Trust, 1974 [1834].

———. *Charity and Its Fruits*. Edinburgh: The Banner of Truth Trust, 1969 [1852].

———. *Jonathan Edwards on Revival*. Edinburgh: The Banner of Truth Trust, 1965 [original date unavailable].

———. *The Religious Affections*. Edinburgh: The Banner of Truth of Trust, 1997 [1746].

Gardiner, J. Norman. *Jonathan Edwards: A Retrospect*. Boston: Houghton, Mifflin and Company, 1901.

Gaustad, Edwin Scott. *The Great Awakening in New England*. Gloucester, Mass.: Peter Smith, 1965 [1957].

Gerstner, Edna. *Jonathan and Sarah: An Uncommon Union*. Morgan, Pa.: Soli Deo Gloria, 1995.

Gerstner, John H. *Jonathan Edwards: A Mini-Theology*. Morgan, Pa.: Soli Deo Gloria, 1996 [1987].

———. *Jonathan Edwards, Evangelist*. Morgan, Pa.: Soli Deo Gloria, 1995 [1960].

Gillies, John. *Historical Collections of Accounts of Revivals*. Edinburgh: The Banner of Truth Trust, 1981 [1754, 1845].

Grosart, Rev. Alexander B., ed. *Selections From the Unpublished Writings of Jonathan Edwards of America*. Ligonier, Pa.: Soli Deo Gloria, 1992 [1865].

Larsen, David L. *The Company of the Preachers: A History of Biblical Preaching From the Old Testament to the Modern Era*. Grand Rapids: Kregel Publications, 1998.

Levin, David, ed. *Jonathan Edwards: A Profile*. New York: Hill and Wang, 1969.

Lloyd-Jones, D. M. *The Puritans: Their Origins and Successors*. Edinburgh: The Banner of Truth Trust, 1987.

McDermott, Gerald R. *One Holy and Happy Society: The Public Theology of Jonathan Edwards*. University Park, Pa.: The Pennsylvania State University Press, 1992.

———. *Seeing God: Twelve Reliable Signs of True Spirituality*. Downers Grove: InterVarsity Press, 1995.

McGiffert, Arthur Cushman, Jr. *Jonathan Edwards*. New York: Harper and Brothers Publishers, 1932.

Murray, Iain H. *Jonathan Edwards: A New Biography*. Edinburgh: The Banner of Truth Trust, 1987.

Piper, John. *God's Passion for His Glory: Living the Vision of Jonathan Edwards*. Wheaton: Crossway Books, 1998.

Simonson, Harold P. *Jonathan Edwards: Theologian of the Heart*. Grand Rapids: William B. Eerdmans Publishing Company, 1974.

Smith, John E. *Jonathan Edwards: Puritan, Preacher, Philosopher*. Notre Dame: University of Notre Dame Press, 1992.

Smith, John E., Harry S. Stout, and Kenneth Minkema, eds. *A Jonathan Edwards Reader*. New Haven: Yale University Press, 1995.

Stout, Harry S. *The New England Soul: Preaching and Religious Culture in Colonial New England*. New York: Oxford University Press, 1986.

Thompson, Rev. C. L. *Times of Refreshing, Being a History of American Revivals, With Their Philosophy and Methods*. Rockford, Ill.: Golden Censer Co., 1878.

Tracy, Joseph. *The Great Awakening*. Edinburgh: The Banner of Truth Trust, 1842.

Tracy, Patricia J. *Jonathan Edwards, Pastor: Religion and Society in Eighteenth-Century Northampton*. New York: Hill and Wang, 1979.

Turnbull, Ralph G. *Jonathan Edwards the Preacher*. Grand Rapids: Baker Book House, 1958.

Walker, Williston. *The Creeds and Platforms of Congregationalism*. New York: The Pilgrim Press, 1991 [1893].

Warfield, Benjamin B. *The Works of Benjamin B. Warfield, Vol. IX: Studies in Theology*. Grand Rapids: Baker Book House, 1991.

Wesley, John. *The Works of John Wesley*, 14 vols. Grand Rapids: Baker Book House, 1979.

Whitefield, George. *George Whitefield's Journals, 1737–1741*. Florida: Scholars' Facsimiles & Reprints, 1969.

Notes

Chapter 1

1. Arnold Dallimore, *George Whitefield*, vol. 1 (Edinburgh: The Banner of Truth Trust, 1970), 413.
2. Sydney E. Ahlstrom, *A Religious History of the American People* (New Haven: Yale University Press, 1973), 281.
3. Iain H. Murray, *Jonathan Edwards: A New Biography* (Edinburgh: The Banner of Truth Trust, 1987), 18.
4. Ibid., 89.
5. David Levine, ed., *Jonathan Edwards: A Profile* (New York: Hill and Wang, 1969), 95.
6. Jonathan Edwards, *The Works of Jonathan Edwards*, 2 vols. (Edinburgh: The Banner of Truth Trust, 1834 [1974]), 1:349. Hereafter referred to as *Works*.
7. *Works*, 1:210
8. Ibid., 1:12.
9. Ibid.
10. "Personal Narrative" in John E. Smith, Harry S. Stout, and Kenneth Minkema, eds., *A Jonathan Edwards Reader* (New Haven: Yale University Press, 1995), 282.

Chapter 2

1. Murray, 26.
2. *Works*, 1:18.
3. Murray, 31.
4. Ibid., 64.
5. Benjamin B. Warfield, *The Works of Benjamin B. Warfield*, vol. 9 (Grand Rapids: Baker Book House, 1991), 530.
6. *Personal Narrative*, 283.
7. Ibid., 284.
8. Ibid.
9. Ibid., 285.
10. Ibid.
11. Ibid., 285–86.
12. *Works*, 1:20–22.
13. Murray, 46.
14. *Personal Narrative*, 286–87.
15. Ibid., 287–88.
16. "Diary" in Smith, et al., 268.
17. Murray, 44.
18. *Personal Narrative*, 289.
19. Smith, et al., say the month was July. See p. 279, note 2.
20. Ahlstrom, 299.
21. *Personal Narrative*, 290–91.
22. *Works*, 1:32.

Chapter 3

1. Henry Wadsworth Longfellow, from "The Village Blacksmith," *Complete Poems of Longfellow* (New York: The Modern Library, n.d.), 622.
2. "Faithful Narrative" in Smith, et al., 58.
3. *Works*, 1:132.
4. Patricia J. Tracy, *Jonathan Edwards, Pastor: Re-*

ligion and Society in Eighteenth-century North-
ampton (New York: Hill and Wang, 1979), 20.
5. Murray, 79.
6. Ibid., 89.
7. *Works*, 1:39.
8. "Apostrophe" in Smith, et al., 281.

Chapter 4

1. Murray, 94.
2. Samuel Hopkins in Levine, 40.
3. Murray, 312.
4. For a detailed analysis of Edwards as a preacher,
   see Ralph G. Turnbull, *Jonathan Edwards the
   Preacher* (Grand Rapids: Baker Book House,
   1958).
5. *Works*, 1:955ff.
6. See Smith, et al., 35ff.
7. Murray, 142.
8. *Works*, 2:955ff.
9. *Personal Narrative*, 292–93.
10. Ibid., 294.
11. Ibid.
12. Ahlstrom, 300.
13. *Works*, 2:6.
14. Hopkins in Levine, 41.
15. D. M. Lloyd-Jones, *The Puritans: Their Origins
    and Successors* (Edinburgh: The Banner of Truth
    Trust, 1987), 356.
16. *Works*, 2:17.
17. Ibid., 1:347.
18. Ibid., 2:620ff.
19. Ibid., 1:347.
20. Ibid., 1:63

Chapter 5

1. *Works*, 1:620.
2. *Faithful Narrative*, 12–13.
3. Ibid., 24.
4. Ibid., 14.
5. Ibid., 44.
6. Ibid., 37–38, 45.
7. Ibid., 45–47, 72.
8. Edwin Scott Gaustad, *The Great Awakening in New England* (Gloucester, Mass.: Peter Smith, 1965), 18–20.
9. Murray, 150.
10. Ibid.
11. Ibid., 120.
12. Ibid., 121, notes that "New Hampshire" should read "Hampshire."
13. Ahlstrom, 283.
14. John Wesley, *The Works of John Wesley*, 14 vols. (Grand Rapids: Baker Book House, 1979), 1:160. Journal entry for October 9, 1738.

Chapter 6

1. From the introduction to "The Distinguishing Marks of a Work of the Spirit of God," in *Jonathan Edwards on Revival* (Edinburgh: The Banner of Truth Trust, 1995 [1741]), 78. Hereafter referred to as "Distinguishing Marks."
2. Joseph Tracy, *The Great Awakening* (Edinburgh: The Banner of Truth Trust, 1842), 8.
3. Dallimore, 493.
4. Ibid., 434–35.
5. Ibid., 481–82.
6. George Whitefield, *George Whitefield's Journals*,

1737–1741 (Florida: Scholars' Facsimiles and Reprints, 1969), 407–08.

7. Ibid., 421.
8. Murray, 163.
9. "An Account of the Revival of Religion in Northampton in 1740–1742" in *Jonathan Edwards on Revival*, 149. Hereafter referred to as "Account."
10. "Account," 149.
11. Ibid., 150.
12. "Sinners in the Hands of an Angry God" in Smith, et al., *A Jonathan Edwards Reader*, 89–105. Hereafter referred to as "Sinners."
13. Murray, 169.
14. "Sinners," 105.
15. Murray, 168–69.
16. "Account," 151.
17. "Distinguishing Marks," 91.
18. Ibid., 109–16.
19. Ibid., 130.

Chapter 7

1. *Works*, 1:62–68.
2. "Account," 153–54.
3. Ibid., 154.
4. Ibid., 158–59.
5. Ibid., 160.
6. Gaustad, 36.
7. Ibid., 39.
8. Tracy, 242.
9. Ibid., 248–49.
10. See Ahlstrom, 285; Gaustad, 36ff.; and Tracy, 230ff.
11. Murray, 205.
12. Ibid., 238.

13. See Section IV of *Some Thoughts Concerning the Present Revival*.
14. "Account," 154–58.
15. Jonathan Edwards, *The Religious Affections* (Edinburgh: The Banner of Truth Trust, 1997 [1746]), 15.
16. Ibid., 266.
17. Ibid., 294.
18. Ibid., 188.
19. Ibid., 120, italics added.

Chapter 8

1. *Works*, 1:115.
2. Murray, 142.
3. Hopkins in Levine, 44.
4. Murray, 192.
5. Ibid.
6. Ibid., 293.
7. Ibid., 294.
8. *Works*, 1:61.
9. Ibid., 2:306.
10. Ibid., 2:315.
11. Ibid., 1:64.
12. Arthur Cushman McGiffert, *Jonathan Edwards* (New York: Harper and Brothers Publishers, 1932), 124–25.
13. Ibid., 125.
14. *Works*, 1:198.
15. Ibid., 1:432.
16. Murray, 321–22.
17. Ibid., 327.
18. *Works*, 1:198.
19. Murray, 328.

Chapter 9

1. *Works*, 1:120.
2. Murray, 356.
3. Ibid., 357.
4. Ibid., 363.
5. McGiffert, 146.
6. Murray, 378.
7. *Works*, 1:153.
8. Alexander B. Grosart, ed., *Selections From the Unpublished Writings of Jonathan Edwards of America* (Ligonier, Pa.: Soli Deo Gloria, 1992 [1865]), 191ff.
9. John Smith, *Jonathan Edwards: Puritan Preacher, Philosopher* (Notre Dame: University of Notre Dame Press, 1992), 63.
10. John H. Gerstner, *Jonathan Edwards: A Mini-Theology* (Morgan, Pa.: Soli Deo Gloria, 1996), 9.
11. *Works*, 1:125.
12. Ibid., 1:127; see Smith, chapter 6.
13. Murray, 434.
14. *Works*, 1:174.
15. Ibid.
16. Ibid., 1:175

Chapter 10

1. *Works*, 1:690–691.
2. McGiffert, 212.
3. *Works*, 1:179.
4. Ibid.
5. McGiffert, 133–34.
6. Tracy, 411.
7. *Works*, 1:125–127.
8. Murray, 464–65.

INTRODUCE YOURSELF TO
ANOTHER HERO OF THE FAITH.

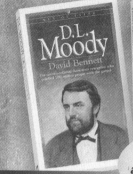

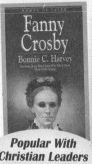

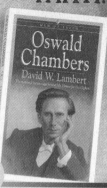

Gathered from across centuries and continents, the biographies in the MEN and WOMEN OF FAITH series all have one thing in common— an inspiring example of a person dedicated to living fully for God. Whether missionary, writer, theologian, or ordinary citizen, each person featured in the series provides us with both encouragement for our own lives as well as an appreciation of our spiritual history.

Often thrilling and always compelling, the MEN and WOMEN OF FAITH biographies ensure that the stories of our Christian heritage will continue to live on.

MEN AND WOMEN OF FAITH
BIOGRAPHIES
Amy Carmichael—1-55661-302-4
Andrew Murray—1-55661-670-8
Borden of Yale—1-55661-014-9
Brother Andrew—1-55661-195-1
C.S. Lewis—1-55661-126-9
Charles Colson—1-55661-629-5
Charles Finney—0-87123-061-5
Charles Spurgeon—0-87123-667-2
Corrie ten Boom—1-55661-194-3
D.L. Moody—1-55661-304-0
David Brainerd—0-7642-2173-6
E.M. Bounds—0-7642-2009-8
Eric Liddell—1-55661-150-1
Florence Nightingale—0-87123-985-X
Francis & Edith Schaeffer—1-55661-843-3
George Muller—0-87123-182-4
Gladys Aylward—1-55661-090-4
Harriet Tubman—0-7642-2182-5
Hudson Taylor—0-87123-951-5
Isobel Kuhn—0-87123-976-0
Jim Elliot—1-55661-125-0
John Calvin—0-7642-2005-5

John & Betty Stam—1-55661-124-2
John Newton—1-55661-305-9
John Paton—1-55661-495-0
John Wesley—0-87123-272-3
Jonathan Goforth—0-87123-842-X
Joni Eareckson Tada—1-55661-364-4
Luis Palau—1-55661-842-5
Madame Guyon—0-7642-2175-2
Martin Luther—1-55661-306-7
Mary Slessor—0-87123-849-7
Oswald Chambers—1-55661-942-1
Samuel Morris—0-87123-950-7
Susanna Wesley—0-7642-2003-9
William Booth—1-55661-307-5
William Carey—0-87123-850-0

Available from your nearest Christian bookstore (800) 991-7747 or from:

BETHANY HOUSE PUBLISHERS

11400 Hampshire Ave. S.,
Minneapolis, MN 55438
www.bethanyhouse.com